HELLO Darlink!

BARBARA McNAUGHT

Copyright © Barbara McNaught

First published in Australia in 2024
by KMD Books
Waikiki, WA 6169

All rights reserved. No part of this book may be used or reproduced by any means, graphic, electronic, or mechanical, including photocopying, recording, taping or by any information storage retrieval system without the written permission of the copyright owner except in the case of brief quotations embodied in critical articles and reviews.

Because of the dynamic nature of the Internet, any web addresses or links contained in this book may have changed since publication and may no longer be vaild. The views expressed in this work are solely those of the author and do not necessarily reflect the views of the publisher and the publisher hereby disclaims any responsibility for them.

Cover design by Dylan Ingram

Cover image - Robbie Merritt.

Typeset in Adobe Garamond Pro 12.5/18pt

 A catalogue record for this work is available from the National Library of Australia

National Library of Australia Catalogue-in-Publication data:

Hello Darlink / Barbara McNaught

ISBN: 978-0-6459479-0-8
(Paperback)

This book is dedicated
TO THOSE
WHO SAY
Hello Darlink!
to LIFE

CONTENTS

PERTH 1
POLAND 9
VIENNA 19
MUNICH, GERMANY 25
ESCAPE FROM A SERIAL KILLER 32
MUNICH – SYDNEY 35
YUGOSLAVIA – HAJKA 42
ROMAN POLANSKI 51
VIENNA – PARIS 55
ARRIVING IN PARIS – FRENCH CONNECTION 60
OMAR SHARIF 67
PARIS – PART 2 71
DOUGLAS – A LOVE STORY! 79
SOUTH AFRICA – MY BABIES 87
SOUTH AFRICA – NEW LIFE 95
BELLE OF THE BALL 107
INSPIRATIONAL WOMEN 120
SAY HELLO DARLINK! TO LIFE 127
BARBARA NIELSEN 135

Can- Can for Canteen

Introduction

PERTH

Arriving in Perth gave me a sense of freedom and safety I hadn't experienced in a very long time.

Driving from the airport after a night flight, arriving in the morning with my two children, I didn't feel like I was on a different continent. I saw the colourful jacarandas and bougainvillea, just like in South Africa, and I remember thinking; *this is weird. I thought it would feel so different, but it doesn't.* I guess, partly because Australia and Africa used to be connected as one continent many of millions of years ago! The first night we slept in our best friend's house and when I woke, I heard the strange call of the crows. I thought it was the husband fighting with his wife, because it sounded to me like an old man being angry!

While my husband had to stay in South Africa for a short time closing up our affairs, our beautiful friends helped me to find a place to rent in Perth. Though, we weren't able to recreate the same wealthy lifestyle we had in South Africa, it felt like heaven. We would go for walks down by the river and eat take-away fish and chips!

Because we left South Africa so quickly, I still had a large outstanding sponsorship deal of R250,000 pending for the National School of the Arts which I had been fundraising for. I remember sitting on the heavenly plush carpet in our new home, (because we hadn't yet got any furniture) and making the call to the prospective donor bank manager in South Africa; 'Don't worry Barbara,' he said, 'the funds have been approved and will be deposited into the school's bank account within ten days. The line is so strange, you sound like you are in Australia, ha ha.' He didn't know I really was calling from Australia until I rang again to thank him once the school had safely received the funds!

We no longer had a huge mansion with a driver and a maid, but I will never regret the move for one day, one hour, one minute or one second. Possessions mean nothing when you don't have your freedom.

I guess I've always been good at moving forward, honouring the transition and embracing a new life and location with no regrets. No matter where you are, I believe you create your own energy for life.

Something that has resonated with me and stayed with me all these years, was a conversation I overheard from the movie director, Robert Davies, who directed the French drama I acted in when I was pregnant in Johannesburg. One of the crew said, 'Oh my God, Joburg is so boring.' He replied, 'No. You create your own energy whenever you get up in the morning… no matter where you are.' I feel I've always created my own enthusiastic view of life and agree with Robert that we create our own energy. When people say they are 'bored', I do wonder how they might change their perspective.

I know I've always been creative, but arriving in Perth was like switching on a light bulb. As soon as my feet touched Western Australian soil, it was like, *WOW!* And I couldn't switch off – not that I wanted to!

In my opinion, Perth has always been a mecca of creativity, though since we're talking 2001-02, it was a very quiet city when compared to some of the vibrant places I'd lived. I was used to places where people go for drinks after work, where the streets are full of people and the cafés and restaurants are always buzzing, places that are open 24 hours, where nobody tells you breakfast is finished, or you can't have lunch after 3pm. Perth was very limited back then. Of course, Barbara being Barbara, I wanted to meet people. I wanted to dress up and go out, but for a while, it felt like I could just live in a track suit, but not for long.

That's when I had an idea to create Momentum; an organisation where women could dress up, come have lunch and a drink, network and meet new people. There was also an opportunity where women in business, or those who wanted to share their journey, could become a corporate member and promote their businesses. So, I put my high heels on and organised meetings with the GM's of some of Perth's top hotels. The manager at The Sheraton Hotel in Perth, (now Pan Pacific) was very blunt, insisting that if we wanted to get media attention to promote our events, we would have to come up with something creative and different. And it came to me in a eureka moment…. 'so we donate 10% of ticket sales and any money from the raffle to a charity.' I believe that every contribution can make a difference in the world where there is so much of an imbalance between wealth and poverty. 'And we get businesses to donate big prizes for the raffle, so they can get some promotion too.' Remember this was 20 years ago, and very innovative for the time. I asked the Sheraton Hotel about important charities in Australia, and they already had a salary deduction for employees who wanted to donate to CANTEEN.

So, the first charity we worked with was CANTEEN – supporting young people living with cancer.

The word *networking* was also pretty new back then. *Momentum* was born to *Network, Fundraise, Socialise and Promote Your Business*. Because networking was such a novelty in Perth, we ended up with regular articles and promotions in all the local newspapers. The first event was an eye-opening experience.

The lunch was in the form of a buffet at the Origins Restaurant at the Sheraton Hotel, with a capacity of 75 guests. We opened the door, and there were 150 women, all dressed up, waiting to come in. I just closed the door on them! I said to my lovely close friend Dianne and then, business partner, 'Oh my God, I think we've got double the numbers.' Luckily it was a buffet, and we were able to handle it. We had all the media there too; The West Australian, Sunday Times, Community Newspapers, and Holly Wood, who was the most beautiful social writer and journalist in Perth.

I was introduced to Holly Wood by my hairdresser. Just before my first event, she said, 'I've read about all you are doing with your networking event and giving to charity. It sounds really good. You have to call Holly Wood.' I thought she meant Hollywood in LA, so, as a joke, I say, 'Darlink, Hollywood has to call me,' to which she replied, 'Okay, I'll give him your number.'

Hello Darlink!

And Holly Wood actually became one of our biggest supporters. He came to all Momentum events, the first Pink Ribbon Ball, and all the other balls to follow. He passed on from cancer in 2009, and when I went to his funeral, it was so emotional, I broke down. He had prepared his own funeral, every detail down to the music and the red rose he gave to the two-and-a-half thousand people who were there. When they read from his diary, he actually apologised for not being unable to attend the Pink Ribbon Ball that year.

Back at the first networking event, I remember standing and welcoming everyone to the inaugural Momentum Networking event where we fundraise, promote our businesses and create magic. I could feel angels flying in the air.

I continued holding these lunches for about a year, and it was 2003 when a friend mentioned a 'pink ribbon' campaign to promote breast cancer awareness, suggesting we could do a Pink Ribbon Ball to help raise more awareness for the campaign - not exclusive to women though; an unmissable big event where women and their partners could enjoy a fantastic night of entertainment. I introduced myself to the Cancer Council WA and the Pink Ribbon Ball was born.

Running events, though is really hard work! For the first ball, I didn't have a structure where I could pay anyone, let alone myself. I organised the whole event with just the help of a university intern. It really was blood, sweat and tears, along with the constant pressure to sell enough tickets to even cover the cost. With our bigger events and the balls we've held over the following years, the pressure never changed. Even when we had a sponsor, we had to fulfil our obligation towards the costs and naming rights, with an expectation that we would sell enough tickets to make the event a success. We also had to ensure support went to the charity in the way we promised. My advice to anybody who thinks events are an easy thing to do, is that they should go behind the scenes. It's like lots of industries with a high profile; acting, publishing, events – things aren't always as easy as they seem on the surface.

But being the face of the event, the connector, is where I excel. I get to relax, maybe two nights before the event because by then, all the logistics have been finalised. It's now in God's hands in a way. The show must go on. Luckily, public speaking is like my second skin. If I stand in front of 500, 5000 or 50,000 people, it's the same to me. It's like being in front of the camera. And it doesn't matter, they all get the same *Barbara*.

There's just one Barbara who shows up for everyone and that's been true my entire life. This is my story…

Cover for the Polish magazine - Cinema

Polish Cinema magazine cover

Chapter 1
POLAND

Growing up in Warsaw, my childhood memories are nothing but beautiful. These days that seems to be the exception rather than the rule. There are so many people I meet in life who tell their stories of growing up, revisiting the trauma of their lives. For me, despite growing up in Poland under strict communist rule, my only thoughts of my childhood are that it was wonderful and very harmonic.

My father was a high-ranking officer in the Polish military; a handsome and charismatic man, very dedicated to his military work. My mother was a very beautiful, creative woman. As was common in those days, mum was very young when she had me and became a stay at home mum. She was an incredibly talented and inventive dressmaker. In another world, she could have been the Coco Chanel of the Eastern Block!

Her signature look was palazzo pants with a long tunic, which even now is very much in fashion; you can see this look everywhere, and it always brings a smile, as it reminds me of her. She designed tops with her 'signature sleeves', which I saw on the catwalks only 10-15 years ago. She was a trailblazer. When my father went to Moscow, on a two-year educational course organised by the military, Mum made herself some amazing outfits and was actually declined entry to a restaurant in Moscow because she was wearing trousers. That's how times have changed since the 50s. I was still very young when it happened but was told the story in later years.

The education system was good in Poland, and back then, we were expected to learn Russian and another foreign language. I asked why we had to learn to speak Russian … and I can always remember the answer, though not who said it. They said, 'When your Russian brother comes to hug you, you have to know how to say 'no', so he doesn't hug you to death….or worse.'

So, the Russian we all learned was a little against our will, but then we could choose any Western language, which was much more fun. I chose English, always being very ambitious from a young age, wanting to be amongst people and situations that were 'better' than me, I subscribed to learn English at the US embassy. At that time, I was the fiancé of Andrzej Jaroszewicz, the son of the then Polish Prime Minister. I didn't think I was doing anything wrong by going for English lessons at the US embassy, but I was taught very quickly that it wasn't acceptable. My father was called in for an interrogation and the Jaroszewicz family brought me to their office to ask me what I was doing. But then, I did get to learn better English by going there!

The communist regime only really became visible to me when I started modelling and wanted to travel outside of Poland for assignments, especially when I got my first international part in a coproduction. Along with my modelling and acting, I was studying law at the beautiful Warsaw University. I thought one day I might need a backup to my acting profession – a real job, I guess. My aim was to graduate in International Law. While I was blessed to be a very popular photo model for different magazines and brands, as well as getting parts as an actress I never ended up finishing the last two semesters of my degree – my movie life took over!

I got a lot of castings and photoshoots in Poland around that time, which were plenty of fun. Partly because I laughed so much, the camera loved me. I don't know whether it was luck or divine intervention, but it all started one day when I was at the bus stop. A young photographer came up to me. 'Do you mind if I take your photo? We're casting the face of polish cosmetic brand Pollena. Would it be OK if I take your details and include your photo?' When I was 16, I won the contract with Pollena which was like the Polish Estee Lauder. I will always remember my first photo session where I actually got paid. I bought my mum a gift and some flowers, excited that I'd made money from modelling. From there, it started rolling in. I was cast for so many brands and companies. I was just the right face at the right time.

I was blessed at the start of my acting career in Poland to have roles in a few movies and TV productions, working alongside some established film actors.

A funny story I remember, was being cast in a popular weekly TV series in Warsaw, called *Kobra*. It was so popular, everyone would stay in to watch it, and it was talked about by everyone. I got a phone call one day from Polish TV saying, 'we want to offer you a title role in Kobra.' Well, as an 18-year-old being in such a popular show, you can imagine my excitement.

Turns out I was playing the role of 'Kristina'. Kristina comes home, puts on the lights, gets hit on the head by a bad person; close up … Kristina is lying dead. She never comes back.

I remember arriving in the studio and being asked which part I was playing. 'The title role of the episode,' I said expectantly, 'Right,' they said, 'you're here to be the dead body…' That was my first non-speaking part in a title role!

One of the movies I acted in was called *The Anatomy of Love* with popular Polish star, Barbara Brylska. I was acting under Barbara Karska as I hadn't yet changed my name to Barbara Nielsen. I played a blonde, naughty mistress, opposite Barbara Brylska's role as the wife. It was a very involved story, but well-written by talented people. Polish movies were mostly psychological dramas at the time.

It was a really good part to play. In one of the scenes, I'm sitting in bed and the main character is leaving. Just for a moment, you see me topless for a glimpse of the camera … but this picture ended up being plastered all over Poland. The newspapers quoted that the Polish river, Wisla, went to boiling point. The movie became very popular and the Polish film director, Roman Zaluski, got lots of praise and recognition.

I had to have a conversation with my father about 'that' picture! But I really have to thank my parents, as they have never, ever, tried to stop me from doing what I wanted to do. Never. I am so grateful to them and the life lessons they taught me. My mum was never conservative, and though my dad was in a very conservative profession, he was also prepared to take risks. They gave me the inspiration to take risks in my life, not to be fearful and not to rely on logic too much. For much of my life, nothing I've done has ever been logical.

I was starting to get together a fairly good body of work and was extremely proud of some of the roles I'd had, when one day, I got a phone call from a Polish film company, saying, 'Barbara, there's an Egyptian co-production that's going to happen. Zoheir Bakir, the Egyptian producer is here and he's casting for several different parts. He saw your picture and would like you to attend the casting.'

So, this ended up becoming my first and classic 'Me Too', or as I call it, 'B2' moment. I sat in reception, waiting amongst half a dozen other young aspiring actresses. As I walked into his office, Mr. Bakir was sitting behind his desk with a big cigar. To me, it looked like it was about a metre long – a really big cigar! While he was telling me about the movie, the way he was staring felt like he was undressing me with his eyes.

He told me about the part. The leading male character was to be a handsome Egyptian student who travels to Poland to study. He's studying sculpture, and in his studio, he's sculpting a young, beautiful model. I interrupted questioning, 'a *nude* model?' When he nodded, I continued, 'Mr. Bakir. Thank you very much, but that's not for me.' He almost dropped his cigar from his big mouth, and asked, 'Why?'

'Well, I'm a talented actress and my parts are not non-speaking parts. I read the script before I came and I'm sorry to see that the lead female part is already taken, but it is the part I would be most suitable for.' I knew the leading part had been given to a very famous Polish actress, named Irena Karel, who was not much older than me. 'OK,' he says, 'explain to me why you think you would be good for the leading part.'

'I feel I could play the role excellently. Because of the story and what she does, it's the perfect part for me.'

The next day, I received a call and was invited to his hotel, the beautiful Bristol Hotel in the centre of Warsaw. I arrived at the hotel to be told Mr. Bakir was 'doing castings today,' and I was expected *upstairs*. 'He's waiting for you.' I went into his suite. He didn't touch me, but he was touching himself during our conversation. 'The contract is not signed yet with Miss Karel as the leading character,' he said. 'I'm about to call a meeting with the production team, as I think, perhaps you would be more suitable. You have such a confidence and are so beautiful. You're the future Polish Brigitte Bardot,' he continued. 'Lucky for you the contract's not been signed. Yes, the more I think about it, the more I think you could get the leading part.'

At this point, I was literally feeling sick, but I said, 'Mr. Bakir, what's the budget for this movie?' He responded with an enormous figure, equivalent to a $100 million dollar movie in today's world. I don't know where my courage came from, but I said, 'Mr. Bakir, do you really think I would sleep with you to get the leading part? With a budget like that, if you didn't believe I was right for the part, you wouldn't give it to me whether I sleep with you or not. So, I won't sleep with you because, one, I don't sleep around. Two, I have a boyfriend and I'm engaged. And three, I don't need to sleep with anyone to get a part in a movie – I'm a very talented actress. No work is worth it. I either make the movie or I don't make the movie, but I won't sleep with anyone to get the part.'

My adrenalin was pumping, but I remember him saying,

'who taught you to talk like that?' I replied, 'No-one. But I'm going to teach the next generation to do only what they feel is right.' He ended up inviting my parents for dinner and told them, 'Congratulations on how you brought up your daughter. I just want to announce that on Monday she's going to be signed off for the leading part of *The Egyptian in Poland*.' Miss Karel ended up with a secondary part. I guess I became one of her biggest enemies in Poland; she probably thought I slept with the producer to get the part, though I absolutely did not. But it was my first real 'Me Too' moment, with him in his fifties and me in my early twenties.

The good part of the story is that we shot the movie in Zakopane, a beautiful ski resort in the south of Poland. I had to learn belly dancing and there was one scene where I had to strip down to my underwear (bra and panties). This scene had two versions, as we were allowed to shoot it that way for European countries, but not for Egypt, and the script had to be changed. The most amazing premiere of the movie was held in the Egyptian embassy with the Egyptian ambassador.

So, apart from the incident with Mr. Bakir I have very good memories of this movie and a nice photo album that they offered to all actors.

But the story could have been so different.

I think here is a good place to stop and reflect that being an actor can be magical, but particularly at certain stages in life, it can be really hard to make a living with it. The consistency and stress of the unknown, waiting on parts you never get, hoping a special role will turn up, reading parts that you want so badly and then seeing them played by someone else. There are moments when the money is rolling in and then suddenly you have no money, and you never know how long the money will have to last. It's very challenging not being in control of your own destiny. So for anybody who is thinking of going into this world, find something extra that is your bread and butter. Even the thinner slice of bread and little bit of butter will give you the emotional freedom to not cry at night when you didn't get the role you so desperately wanted and put your heart into. Of course, it's not only about money, but you have to consider your own survival and putting food on the table.

I left Poland in 1974 and I can still clearly remember telling my parents.

'By the way, I'm going to live in Vienna,' I said as my mum walked beside me. 'I'm leaving next week.' I was so close to my mum, and only now can I imagine how it was like a knife to her heart.

But when you're so young, you are selfish, driven by your emotions and wherever your life journey takes you. With her typical 'beautiful mum' response, she said, 'really, Basia? Well, I hope you'll be happy. Vienna to Warsaw - it's only a one-and-a-half-hour flight. It's not a huge distance.'

When I was living in Vienna and in Munich, mum would join me for many parties and movie premieres, and travel as often as she could, despite the restrictions in Poland at the time. I have the most beautiful pictures of us together with a selection of famous actors, including Roger Moore. He came for the opening of his latest James Bond movie and my mum was photographed talking to him. The next day, there were headlines in the papers, asking 'who is the mysterious blonde with Roger Moore?'

Hello Darlink!

At least I can say with hand on heart, I was able to provide mum with much joy and entertainment. We remained close until her passing in 2020. I would visit Poland every year and mum would come visit me every year too – no matter where I lived.

My dad also visited me in Vienna in the early days, as well as coming out to South Africa when I lived there, a little later in life. Dad was more dedicated to our family than I had ever realised in my younger days. He chose to step down from his position, or perhaps it was 'early retirement', when my life took a turn as a teenager. After I was married and moved to Vienna, being a photo model and flying all over the world, with my picture on billboards in multiple European countries, the Polish Prime Minister decided *my behaviour* wasn't suitable for the daughter of a high-ranking Polish officer. I had no idea until much later, how my choices had affected his career – but he never once complained to me or even made me aware of it. He was happy for me that I was living such a life.

Polish culture is beautiful, and Poland still holds magical memories for me. The white powdery snow of winter, the delicious food and cold Polish beer with raspberry or cranberry juice in the hot summer, the yearly Chopin concert in Lazienki Royal Park; so many beautiful places and things to do.

On one visit, years later, when I was married with two children and living South Africa, I paid a visit to my old Warsaw University. I walked into the administration office and said, 'Hi, I'm Barbara, Basia Karska.' The lady barely looked up from her typing and said, "I know. You still owe us for a book from the library.'

That was my welcome back. It's like I never left.

In front of the famous PolyColor poster

Chapter 2

VIENNA

Vienna 1974. I was married to a young Christian Nielsen who was a son of the Norwegian Ambassador to Poland. We were married before I left to live in Vienna, and the wedding was held at the Norwegian embassy. Sadly for me, because of my father's political connections, my parents were not able to officially attend the wedding.

I felt blessed to be part of his family and proud for my acting name to become Barbara Nielsen. His parents were very elegant, intelligent and caring people. After the wedding, we quickly moved to Vienna. Chris was studying there and we had a beautiful apartment.

I got plenty of castings and work while I was living in Vienna. I became so very busy, earning incredible money for a young woman. I had sometimes four or five bookings a day, every day of the week. I was booked by agencies for magazines and TV adverts. It was my time to shine as a photo model.

I absolutely love the camera, and the camera loves me. When

I'm in front of the camera I can relax, it doesn't feel like work at all. I had the great fortune to have a wonderful and fabulous person as my agent. His name was Heinz Siebeck.

I had established myself as the face of make-up brand, Poly Colour when one day, I received a phone call from Heinz who said, 'Barbara. They're shooting a commercial in Amsterdam for Poly Colour and they want you to have the first option. They want to do something special. They want to create a look like Marilyn Monroe. They're doing the casting photos next week, so just think about how you can look like Marilyn.' I went and bought a beautiful expensive hard copy book on Marilyn, which helped me to create my makeup and hair for the casting shoot. I ended up getting the part and was flown from Vienna to Amsterdam.

After the shoot in Amsterdam, I called my agent two days later and asked him, 'so can you send me the return ticket? Because, you know, I have to fly back.' And he tells me, 'You had Vienna to Amsterdam and Amsterdam to Vienna. You had a return ticket.' I had accidentally thrown the second part away. He wasn't very happy with me. I found Amsterdam to be the most amazing place. It has a very different energy. People are on a different cloud!

The Poly Colour poster was very successful. It was reproduced all over Vienna too, on huge walls, on the side of buildings and people thought it was the 'real' Marilyn Monroe. Several journalists came to me and said 'Barbara, can we do a story about the picture of Monroe? About it not being the 'real' Monroe, but in fact, that it's Barbara Nielsen, a Polish actress who now lives in Vienna.' It certainly got me a lot of publicity. It also got me an invitation to the incredible Vienna Opera Ball at the Vienna Opera House. It's such a wonderful tradition having been held annually now, since 1935, except for a little time during the war. It's the biggest night of the year in Vienna.

Usually attended by the President, the debutantes dance in beautiful white gowns. With my invitation to attend, I called a very special boutique in Munich called *Sweetheart* to make me a gown. They designed me a beautiful black and silver gown, very fitted, but modest and classy, and promised me it would be the only one. (I actually only threw it out not long ago, and already I regret it.)

As I walked into the ballroom, I was introduced to The Austrian Chancellor, Bruno Kreisky. We were greeting the media, when from another room, actress Catharina Conti joined us. I will never forget the moment I realised we were wearing exactly the same gown. How was it possible? Sweetheart Boutique had to answer for that. Catharina was furious, but I was actually laughing. I said, 'Why are you furious? We're going to make headlines. The same thing happened to Sophia Loren.' I couldn't believe she was so angry. In my eyes, if you can't change it, enjoy it! We ended up on the front page of the Kronen Zeitung; a similar paper to The Australian. It was me on the left, Catharina on the right, and Bruno Kreisky in the middle. So, yes, Sweetheart had something to answer for, and I think we both got a credit note for another gown.

I loved my first experience of living in Vienna. The Vienna traditions of going to the outdoor gardens and drinking wine, hold dear memories for me. In Vienna they drink wine all the time, but they dilute it with water. It's called Spritzer. I love the taste. It goes against all the traditions of wine connoisseurs to put water in good wine, but I still put ice in my wine today.

I had been living in Vienna for about 6 months, when my agent called one day. 'Barbara, I have quite amazing news,' he said. 'They've seen your photo in Germany, in Munich, and they're looking for a leading part for an actress to basically replace Uschi Glas.' Uschi Glas, was an absolute star of the 70s. As a young actress she was in all the big German movies. And they were looking for another new face for Heimat movies. I wasn't very fluent in German at the time, but this was an opportunity I didn't want to miss!

On a movie set

BARBARA NIELSEN
Foto: Constantin/Mangold

Constantin Film autograph photo

Chapter 3

MUNICH, GERMANY

When I arrived in Munich, I was very much *Marilyn Monroe* and pictures of me as *Marilyn* were on posters all over the country. Even in my day-to-day life, I had the Monroe hair – very legally blonde. So, I'm wearing a pink leather coat and pink palazzo leather pants, at the taxi rank waiting for a taxi, with my little notebook in my hands. and I called out to the taxi driver 'Constantin Films please'. I remember the address, because even back then, Constantin film was *the* German film production and distribution company. At the time, it compared to MGM. It was so well known in Germany and still is today.

The taxi arrives just as it's starting to rain, and I'm thinking of my pink coat, not really wanting to get wet. A gentleman is standing in the queue just ahead of me, looking very smart in a black coat. 'You can take my taxi,' he smiles as I thank him and tell the driver I'm heading to Constantin Films for a screentest. The taxi driver knows where it is; everyone in Munich knew where Constantin was! What I remember about that screentest, is that I was reading my part in English while my potential acting partners, were answering in German. My German not being the best, I hadn't learnt the part in German yet. Just as we were finishing the screentest, an assistant came into the studio and says, 'Ms Nielsen, there's a phone call for you.' I was a bit surprised, as I didn't think anyone I knew would be trying to contact me at Constantin. I had arranged a meeting with acting talent agent, Elli Silman, in Munich directly after the screentest. She was the biggest agent in Germany at the time, based in Munich. She took care of all the big international stars, including Horst Buchholz and Senta Berger. She was going to interview me as an up-and-coming actress, and maybe take me onto her books, especially if I got the part in the big movie I was auditioning for. I thought perhaps the phone call may have been from her.

Remember, at that point, I was speaking very little German. I pick up the phone and hear a male voice saying, 'Taxi.' All I could think was that it must have been the taxi driver who brought me to the studio, trying to organise a date. So, I said, 'I'm very sorry. I'm busy. I have a meeting straight after the casting and I don't have time as I'm flying out soon.' Boom. I'm taking another taxi and going to Elli's office.

When I arrived, Elli immediately called the director at Constantin; 'How did she go?' They reply, 'Well, honestly, we don't know. We won't know until Monday or Tuesday, and we'll want to start shooting straight away. But she was pretty amazing. She's fresh and she's different…' Elli asked about my little knowledge of German, to which they replied, 'If she does this picture, it doesn't matter, we're going to dub. We'll let you know as soon as we know.'

Elli turned to me, 'So what are you going to do?' she asks. She was referring to the fact that I only had a one-trip visa into Germany. I was travelling on my Polish passport, living in Austria, and only had a one-entry permit.

I was very unsure what to do. I hadn't thought it through before I'd left Vienna. If I were to fly back to Vienna and then get the part, I would need to wait at least two weeks for a new visa. But I couldn't stay in Munich because my ticket to fly home was for that day, and it wasn't a flexible ticket. It all seemed very complicated. The doorbell rang and Elli asked her secretary to check who was there. I saw it was the man at the taxi stand who had given me his taxi. He says directly to me, 'since you didn't accept my call, I'm here,' and then to Elli, 'My name is Klauke. I had the pleasure of meeting the young lady at the taxi stand and I wanted to take her out for coffee … but she said no.' He smiles at me, while Elli looks a little impatient and says, 'Well, look. Nice meeting you, but we actually have a little problem here to sort out. So… maybe if you want to talk later…' He interrupts, 'well, perhaps I can help with the problem. I can help with a lot of things.'

So, Elli starts with the story of Barbara who will probably get the part in a big movie with Roy Black, but she doesn't know yet. (Roy Black was an absolute idol, singer and movie star in Germany in his heyday!) Barbara lives in Vienna and has a ticket to return there later today, but if the movie starts shooting in Munich on Tuesday, she won't be able to get a visa in time. She really needs a multi-entry visa permit to return to Germany. 'Okay,' he says, 'this is something I *can* help with. Can I use your phone?'

He picks up the phone and dials.... I didn't really understand the conversation with German not being my strong point at the time, but Elli told me about it later. 'Hi. Yeah, it's me. I'm with a beautiful, young, aspiring actress who will probably grace our screens as a leading lady in many German Heimat movies. She's going to be in a movie next week with Roy Black, but she has to fly out tonight and doesn't have a return visa. Ok… Danke.' He immediately turned to me with a dazzling smile and said, 'all resolved. I'll take you to the airport. You leave your passport with me and then you can collect your passport on Monday morning back in Vienna, with a multi-entry visa to Germany.' 'You mean I'll be flying without a passport,' I say, incredulous. 'Yes. Don't worry, I'll be there. It will all be cool.' I had a little time to kill before my flight, so we walked and talked together and saw a little of Munich before I had to leave. I was talking all about what Barbara talks about; my husband, my study and work. He took me to the airport, and I arrived back in Vienna without a passport. Before I left, I asked for his number, 'in case I needed any more favours,' and I can clearly remember his name and number written in my notepad.

I don't know who he had spoken to, but I left my passport with him in Munich and arrived in Vienna, no problem. Everybody let me through. I picked up my passport in Vienna on Monday morning, which contained my multiple-visit visa to Germany. On Tuesday morning I heard I had the leading part in the movie and two days later, I flew back to Munich. When I had returned to Munich, I phoned him to say a big 'thank you', but the operator at the number he left said, 'Who? Mr. Klauke? Sorry, we don't know any Mr. Klauke.' Obviously, he must have been a secret agent seeing what Barbara Nielsen was up to!

When we were shooting the movie *Alter Kahn und Junge Liebe*, Old Barge and Young Love, I was the love interest of Roy Black, who was singing in the movie. We were shooting in some of the most beautiful parts of Germany, and had many premieres across Europe, with crowds of fans, because Roy Black was so famous. It was my first big German movie, and I wasn't known at all, but within the first year of being in Germany, I became the second most popular actress there. I think Claudia Cardinale was ahead of me, but that was cool with me; I mean, she was an international star. I was on the covers of all the German magazines, and when we were touring for the opening, there would be a few thousand young people, mostly women, screaming at the train station. One time, we were walking, and a young lady was holding on to Roy asking for his autograph. Somebody in the crowd pushed her, and she actually broke her leg.

When we arrived at our hotel a few hours later, she was sitting at reception with her leg in plaster, asking us to autograph it! My memories of premieres and so many movies I made in a short time in Germany, are amazing.

So, after the first movie, *Alter Kahn und Junge Liebe*, was so successful and opened in all leading cinemas in Germany in 1974, I was offered the opportunity of a lifetime; an exclusive contract with Constantin Film over three years, with three leading parts each year. So, nine leading roles over three years – guaranteed!

I was so excited. I found a telephone box near to Constantin and called my close family friend, Artur Brauner; he was actually a good friend of my mum's. Artur was the founder of CCC Studios and made iconic international movies. He was one of the biggest German producers. He only left this world in 2019 at the proud age of 100-years-old. When you sent a card to Artur Brauner, Berlin, it always arrived; that's how famous he was. I phoned him and said, 'Artur, I need your advice. Constantin Film have offered me an exclusive contract for three movies a year. For three years.' He says, 'So what's the question? They don't offer things like this. This is unbelievable Barbara, just grab it.' He went on to tell me the last contract like mine was offered to Elke Sommer in around 1969. 'It means they're going to help you make your career in movies.'

When I think about it now, it's crazy. I got the leading part without even speaking the language. I was dubbed in *Alter Kahn und Junge Liebe*, and then I was offered the Constantin film contract. Nobody cared which language I did or didn't speak. They just wanted my presence. I was obviously doing *something* right. I got a photo session, sponsored and arranged by Constantin Film, with iconic photographer, Guido Mangold. We went to a country retreat, and he photographed me for two or three days. Just me! The photos have such magic, the whole experience was incredible. I have a whole book of Guido Mangold photos. They were used everywhere in Germany, in Stern magazine and Variety, whenever they were doing an article on my next movie.

The photos were used in cinemas too. In every German cinema, there was a Barbara Nielsen photo because of all the movies I was making. My mailbox would be full of letters requesting autographs, and I'd have them spread 3 layers thick across the table. I remember actually crying because I didn't have time to answer them all. When I travelled, I took some of the unanswered letters with me so I could answer them during the quiet

Hello Darlink!

times when I was filming. I had a whole suitcase filled with my fan post. In those days it was very popular for fans to send letters.

Amsterdam location with Roy Black

Chapter 4

ESCAPE FROM A SERIAL KILLER

There was also another angle for being in the limelight. On my return to Munich from a four week shoot in Strasburg, one of the first things I did was listen to my answering machine, - remember this was before smart phones. I found one, two, three messages from police to call back.

At first I thought I must have driven through a red traffic light, or something similar. But after listening to message number seven, I finally called back.

I was asked to be at the police station next morning at 8am.

When I walked in I was escorted to the private interview room with a sign on the door Criminal Police. When a very polite and measured plain clothes detective thanked me for coming and offered me coffee, I knew this wasn't any traffic fine. He showed me a photo of a well-presented man, asking if I recognised him.

I replied maybe but wasn't sure. He said this man introduced himself as multiple indentities including: diplomat, movie producer, business man etc.

I was also shown a photo of a dark haired woman whom I couldn't recall meeting.

Next the detective presented me with a hand written diary with my name address, telephone number and a note with the date of an article in a local newspaper about my next movie part including a glam photo of me.

The penny dropped and I froze!

A couple of weeks prior my departure for filming I found every morning a fresh rose behind my car windscreen in the underground parking,.

Honestly I didn't pay much attention to it, thinking this was just another fan.

The diary turned out to have belonged to a serial killer, who together with his female accomplice had murdered four young blonde women by then. My name was next on their list.

Me being away on the shoot probably saved my life.

Everything is timing ! and...

There's no business like show business.

Still from Tully

Stills from Tully with Jack Thompson and Tony Valentine

Chapter 5

MUNICH – SYDNEY

I was extremely lucky to have Elli Silman as my agent; she was a bit like a step-mum to me while I lived in Munich. One day I had a sore tooth, so Elli got me an appointment with her dentist. I was sitting in the dentist chair waiting for him to give me a numbing injection so he could pull a tooth, when the phone rang. It's Elli and she says, 'Can I please speak to Barbara?' The dentist replies, 'Well, she's just about to have her procedure done.' I could hear her say, 'NO, stop, I have to talk to her…' To cut a long story short, she says, 'Barbara, there's an Australian English producer-director here in Munich. They're here casting for a leading part in a TV series for ABC Sydney, and they want to see you. Can you meet them now in the Konigshof Hotel? It's right across the road from where you are at the dentist!'

So I left the dentist, without fixing my tooth, and sat down in front of the casting director and the movie director. 'We have a casting session tomorrow we'd like you to attend. If it goes well, could you fly to Sydney next week? On Tuesday?' Hello!

Everything I did in the early stages of my career seemed to happen so quickly. I guess that's show business. So, the following day, I read the part at the casting …. and I got the part! Now I needed a visa to fly to Sydney the following Tuesday. So, I went to the Australian Embassy with Elli, and it's 4.45pm on Friday afternoon; the embassy closes in 15 minutes.

The officer is vetting me and checking I don't have a criminal history. I promise him, 'I won't stay in Sydney forever. I will be back. It's just a job.' I show him the document from the film company that says I will be employed in Sydney for three months. He says, 'So where's your passport photo?' Oh my God, nobody told me I needed a passport photo. 'Don't you have a passport photo machine?' I ask. Remember, this is the mid-70s. He tells me I have to go to the post office to get the photo, so he can't do the visa today. Then I remembered something; 'You know what?' I said. 'Today in the newspaper is a whole page photo of me. It's a bikini photo, but we can cut the head off and maybe use that for the passport photo.' He laughs and says, 'alright, but only if I can keep the rest? Maybe you can autograph it for me.' That's how I got my Australian visa and first flew to Sydney.

The part I was playing opposite the very well-known rising star, Jack Thompson voted sexiest man alive, trending with his famous Cleo centerfold. Jack Thompson played my lover, while Tony Valentine, an English actor, played my boyfriend.

The night before I flew to Sydney, I was invited by Constantin Film to a big Gala Dinner, and because I was under contract, I had to attend. I was seated next to a distinguished gentleman, who was from 20th Century Fox in Los Angeles, California.

He says, 'Congratulations. I heard you are flying to Sydney

Hello Darlink!

for three months with the leading part opposite Jack Thompson.' 'Yes,' I said, 'I'm very excited.' 'Well, I live in LA, but I'd like to support you,' he said. 'What I'll do is send a cable to the 20th Century Fox office in Sydney, just in case you need anything.' I was so overwhelmed by the kindness of someone I'd only just met!

It's a long way from Munich to Sydney, but even longer back then. I was flying from Munich to Paris, then from Paris to Singapore, and Singapore to Sydney, with amazing French airline UTA, sadly no longer in operation. My partner in the movie, Tony Valentine, was flying London to Paris, before meeting up and flying the rest of the way with me to Sydney. When he arrived, he was wearing a dark navy Hugo Boss suit. The fantastic suit he was wearing was actually one of the production costumes. He'd been doing a dress rehearsal in London but loved it so much, he decided to wear it on the flight. It did look very elegant!

During the flight, he told me his wife would be following in five days but had to get permission to fly as she was 7 months pregnant. Halfway through, he quickly got up from his seat looking distressed. Turns out, he had somehow got chewing gum on his trousers. 'What am I going to do?' he says to the stewardess. There was an attempt by stewardesses to remove the gum from between his legs with cold or hot water, but it didn't work. All best efforts failed to remove the gum. Okay, now I'm giving a hot tip. Somebody comes up from the seat behind and says, 'guys, there's only one thing that takes chewing gum off, and that's peanut butter.' And it worked!

The first-class flight was unforgettable, particularly as the captain invited me to the cockpit as we were landing in Singapore that night. I'll never forget watching the twinkling of the lights as we prepared to land. He offered me a glass of champagne and I was concerned as he was more interested in talking to me than flying the plane! I pointed this out to him, but he said, 'Don't worry, everything is automated, I don't have to touch anything.' (Even back then!) It was an unforgettable moment.

We arrived in Singapore, and I checked in to a huge suite at the famous Raffles Hotel. When I woke the next day, I called room service asking, 'May I have breakfast, please?' They said, 'Mrs … breakfast time is over.' 'OK. Can I have lunch then, please? I'm exhausted and don't really want to go out yet.' 'Well,' he continues, 'lunch is over too. We can offer you afternoon tea.' I was shocked; 'What time is it?' It was 4.15pm and the plane to Sydney was leaving at 6.30pm - I had to rush to the airport. That's how much I saw of Singapore that day, from the beautiful Raffles Hotel.

After another long flight, we arrived in Sydney and I checked in to my hotel.

As soon as I arrived, in my room was a huge basket of fruits with a greeting card from 20th Century Fox. 'Welcome to Sydney. If you need anything, we'd love to assist you.' As I looked around at the beautiful hotel, I wondered how I might need their help. Everything was first class because ABC was very generous, and it was a well-paying production.

They had brought me to Sydney almost three weeks in advance, for publicity, wardrobe, make-up and hair, for rehearsals, and for getting me into the atmosphere of Sydney. Little did I know, at the time, that I would be living in Australia so many years later. Unfortunately, the hotel where I was staying had no restaurant downstairs, and as the crew were all Australian, I didn't have a crew to hang out with at the hotel either. Usually when you shoot a movie, you're with a crew most of the time, but not there. I hadn't met my acting partner Jack Thompson yet, and my co-partner, Tony Valentine, had hired a house on the beach because his pregnant wife had permission to fly and was soon to join him. So, there I was, quite lonely and with no one to talk to. We had rehearsals and meetings during the day, but then you come home to your hotel and what do you do? How do you go for dinner on your own in Sydney? So, I phoned Richard Harper at 20th Century Fox to thank him for the beautiful welcome and to ask if he might be able to help me find another hotel, with a bit more to do, that the production would be agreeable to.

And they found me a new hotel with a swimming pool and restaurants. They also endorsed me as a VIP in the who's who club of Sydney Entrepreneurs VIP Club. I was celebrating my birthday in September in the most beautiful restaurant. I can still remember the stars in the sky that night. I spent three magical months in Sydney, and I remember thinking, 'this is as close to Hollywood as you can get' - without actually being in Hollywood! I had my own caravan on set and my own chair with *Barbara Nielsen* written on it. I was always picked up for my shooting days, as well as being consulted and prepared every step of the way. It was the most professional production.

I met Jack Thompson, a few days down the road when we were shooting scenes together, and he was a most open and free person, living at the time with two sisters, as a 'triple' not a couple! My first impression of Sydney was, 'my God, people are so happy here.'

Does anybody ever stay home in Sydney and cook dinner alone? It seemed to me that everyone goes out all the time and people put on their dancing shoes and love to go dancing in Sydney.

When I flew home to Munich, I remember saying to my friends, 'you know, guys, if you think Australia is behind Europe, you're making a big mistake. Australia rocks.'

Many years later, destiny brought me back to Australia and I tried to contact Jack. It would have been an absolute honour and incredible if I could have interviewed him for my Hello Darlink! show. I haven't been lucky yet, but I will keep trying!

Tully in Sydney newspaper article

Hajka movie- Yugoslavia

Chapter 6
YUGOSLAVIA – HAJKA

Constantin Film informed me I had been asked to go to a casting for a co-production movie; a war story to be shot in Yugoslavia. During a meeting with the producer and director, they told me the story of the character I'd be auditioning for. 'Barbara,' they said, 'can you fly next week to Belgrade for a screen test?' They gave me the script, and as I'm reading I'm wondering, *why me?* The character was described as a very tall, country woman. She's nine months pregnant and the father of her child is a soldier from the opposition. I was confused as to why they wanted me. Physically, I wasn't right for the part, and I'd recently read about this movie in the papers; I read they were casting a leading Yugoslavian actress for the part, a really big star.

But I'm flying to Belgrade, of course, for the casting. In the make-up room, they sprayed my hair dark brown and pulled it all tightly back. They dressed me for the part too; war clothes, big tummy, very sparse make up.

So, the opening scene during the casting was a difficult one.

It was when the character finds out she can't see the father of her child. It was a very emotional scene, and you must be on a journey for a while to be able to deliver it well. So, I'm doing the scene when the director comes in. His name was [Zika Pavlović](), a very famous published author and script writer. I'll never forget his words to me that day. He said, 'What's wrong?' He held his hands far apart, gesturing as he spoke. 'This is the character, and this is you. You are now so far from each other. I chose you to audition because, I know you can give me this.' I guess I was feeling way out of my depth with this character. I'd met the other actress who was auditioning, while we were in the dressing room, and felt she already had the part. You've probably gathered by now that I can be pretty blunt, so I said, 'I think I'll finish up now because I know you're casting the other actress.' He said, 'Listen … do you think we would waste our money, my time and your time, to bring you all the way to Belgrade if we couldn't see the character in you? You are her. You just haven't delivered her to us yet. We have to see you being her. And then we talk.'

So, I put on my best performance and got the leading part. We shot for three months in Yugoslavia in the mountains. And when they shot the close-ups, I was speaking Serbian, and although I can't speak the language, being Polish, it was easy for me. I will never forget it.

When my partner came to visit me, I would go out with him in the evening in my suede leggings, knee-high boots, brushed off blonde hair and big sweater. In the morning, I would go to breakfast, dressed and ready for filming with my big tummy and dark hair. I laughed when I heard someone at the hotel say, 'this bastard guy … he's here having breakfast in the morning with his pregnant wife but spends his evenings with a beautiful blonde.'

The movie won a prize at the festival in Pula, Italy. I remember the credits described me as a German star, though I still didn't speak German very well so they were all a bit confused; 'how can she be German with the way she speaks Serbian?'

I'm going to digress a little here with an amazing story about how small the world is. I have never seen my movie, *Hajka*. By the time it went out into German cinemas, I was living in Paris. I was frantically busy, just moving on. I never saw the movie and on the few occasions many years later when I tried to Google it, I just never got around to watching it.

I hadn't been living in Perth for long, when I was strolling in the shopping centre in South Perth and went into a beautiful little store called *Pearls In The City* where I met a gorgeous lady, Liljana, who was the owner, and we started chatting. She's from Yugoslavia and says, 'my husband is from Croatia and his dad was an actor years ago.' 'Really? What movies? Because I made a movie in Yugoslavia,' I reply. 'He was very famous,' she says, 'a big star. His name was Milos Kandic. One of his movies was called Hajka.' Her father-in-law, a big Yugoslavian film star, played the opposition general in the movie I was in. We never met on set because we were never filming together, shooting on different days and different locations, but I ended up meeting his family many years later in Perth. I guess it was meant to be.

I recall the fun we had on set, and the pretend baby I was carrying in the movie, everyone making the jokes; 'Is it a boy or a girl?'

Where we were filming in the countryside, I recall a gorgeous little local boy, named Marco, maybe three years old. He would watch us on set while we were filming. I remember looking at his dirty clothes, and him picking up apples from the floor and eating them. He looked a picture of health, rosy cheeks and bright blue eyes. My memory of that is thinking, 'My gosh, how we care for our babies these days. We disinfect everything. Even disinfect our breath before we kiss them. This is a boy in the countryside, eating from the floor, shoes with holes, looking the very picture of health you can imagine and beaming with joy.

Obviously, a lot of things I say here in my book, are just my observations, I'm not recommending anything, but I wonder if we are decreasing our own immune system with the things we're doing to ourselves. I think life is supposed to get messy!

So, this was my Yugoslavian adventure, while I was living in Germany. The area where we shot Hajka was called Golden Boar, which means Golden Forest. It was so wonderful; such a beautiful country and beautiful people as well. A healthy, vital and simple existence.

I feel blessed to have experienced so many different cultures. When I travel back to the countries where I have lived, like when I arrive in Vienna, my mouth is watering as I'm craving for a pastry that I used to eat regularly. Or when I'm visiting in Munich, I'm craving for Pretzels and Sauerkraut. When I get back to some of those places, within a day or two I start to dream in those languages. Honestly, I will wake up and talk to my husband Douglas in another language. It's incredible.

Another fabulous memory from my time in Germany, was when I was cast in a very famous TV weekly serial drama, called Derrick. I played a female part in a few episodes, with my own accent. The response from the public to my character was great because everybody was watching the show every week, and I was being recognised for the part, where I played a foreign glamorous, young agent. It was an interesting experience.

Being so young when living in Germany, I probably wasn't aware of what a privilege it was for me to be working so much as a young actress who didn't even speak German fluently, (I do now.) And having a contract with Constantin Film gave me unbelievable security because I got paid for three leading parts a year over those three years. After Elli retired, my follow up agent was Janusz Pilecki. I remember some of the first words he said to me; 'Are you aware how lucky you are? Barbara, your salary is more than what most families with two or three kids live on. You've got to create a lifestyle that's sustainable.' But I don't think I really heard him at the time. My pictures were in every German cinema, and I was recognised everywhere I went.

One day I was offered a part in a French TV series production called The Chameleon Lady, the famous classic. Even though I'd been offered the part I had to go for the official casting. Europe does that! You have to be there in person, so they have a record of you and how you project the part and the character, regardless of how well-known and professional you are, or how many movies you've made.

I bought myself a new car so I could drive to the casting. But how did anyone go about buying a new car in the 70s without the internet? I still don't know much about cars today. The car was a red, second-hand Fiat X19, but I got it at a good price. I met the person who was selling the car, literally in front of my flat. I looked at it, gave him the money and got straight in to drive to the casting in Cologne. So, here's Barbara wearing a Marilyn

Monroe dress, and looking like MM with my make-up and hair, because I'd just done some publicity for Poly Colour and I didn't have time to change.

I was driving and already outside of Munich when I realised I didn't really know how to get to the city of Cologne. There was no GPS then, after all. I'm driving on the highway and in Germany, there's no speed limit. You can drive at 300kph and nobody will stop you. I'm in my new X19, doing say 120kph, and suddenly it goes down in speed - 110, 80, 90. I push the accelerator, but it just stops. I'm standing on the side of a highway in my Monroe shoes and dress. Obviously, I didn't stand for long, when a Mercedes stopped. I tell the driver my car doesn't drive, and he wants to take a look at the engine. But it's not in the front, so it must be in the back, right? He opens the back - no engine. He says, 'how long have you owned the car?' 'About an hour,' I said. 'Well,' he replied, 'you've actually come very far without an engine!' Turns out the Fiat X19 had what's called a middle engine, between the boot and the back seat; a very small engine. My car had to be towed away.

Luckily, I was a member of the roadside assistance in Germany and another car was delivered so I could continue on my drive to the casting. I arrived in Cologne in a Volkswagen Beetle. I got the part, and The Chameleon Lady was shot in Bordeaux. That was another magical experience with some very big German and Austrian stars. Watching the set transform from a modern place to one from another century, and the exquisite costumes we wore, was a fantastic experience. Meeting Erika Pluhar, a very famous actress, was also an interesting experience for me; understanding that many big stars are very introverted in their private lives. Their talent as an actor transforms them into different personalities and personas.

I also had a part in a stage play in the theatre in Germany. The transition from camera actor to stage actor was a wonderful learning curve for me. On stage, everything has to be 'bigger'. In front of the camera, acting works in a different way. Nothing escapes the camera, but also things appear differently on camera. Very often when we see a big star we know from the screen, and then see them in person, we think, 'oh, he's so much smaller,' or 'she's so much thinner.' The camera can make things appear differently, however when you're an intuitive actor, the camera can see the subtle differences and the viewer sees it too. Some actors are luckier than others to have that presence on screen.

My stage experience came about as part of a drama training course I was doing to keep working on my skills and improving myself. I feel strongly that we should all learn more, do more and be more, to keep growing and developing our knowledge and skills in our lives.

One time, I had been confirmed for a major part in a German/Italian co-production. I'd been to rehearsals, had fittings for costumes, make-up and hair. The newspapers had already written about the production and how I was to be the star. That's when I got the phone call. 'Barbara, we don't have good news. Unfortunately, the co-production has been restructured, it's going to be a German/British production, and they have decided to cast a British female lead. The lead is not your part anymore.' The part went to Britt Ekland, and she's not even British!

I became very upset and depressed. I was so serious; actually, that's a better word. I didn't have my contract with Constantin

Hello Darlink!

Films by then, and I realised I'd had enough. Enough of waiting for parts every day, desperately listening to my answering machine to hear about castings and parts I wanted. It was time to get a normal job, but what would I do? I'd never had a normal job before. I called a friend in Vienna. 'I've had enough,' I said. 'What can you do to help me get a normal job?'

So, I returned to Vienna – but first, I must tell you about my wonderful friendship with Roman Polanski!

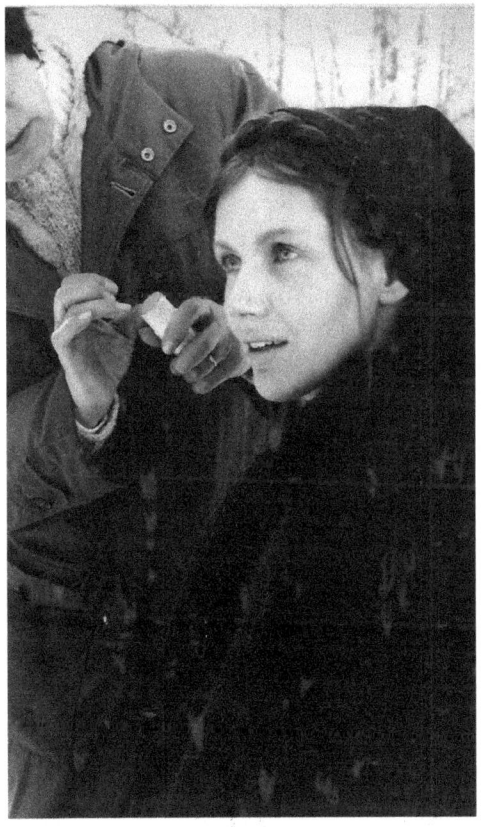

On set of the Hajka movie in Yugoslavia

With Roman Polanski at the Spoleto festival in Italy.

Chapter 7
ROMAN POLANSKI

I've mentioned before that Elli Silman was very special to me. For the first three months when she took me on as her client, I didn't have place to live yet, having moved from Vienna to Munich. I ended up renting a room with Elli until I found my own place. One day she said, 'One of my clients, a very famous TV presenter, is moving to Hamburg and her place will be perfect for you.' It was a two-bedroom apartment, with an underground garage and a sauna and swimming pool in the building. I moved in within three months of arriving in Munich to film my first German movie *Alter Kahn und Junge Liebe*, and I loved living there.

But staying with Elli was quite an experience. She worked from home, which is normal today, but very different in those days. One day she said, 'Barbara, darling. I think we should write to Roman Polanski. He has to know about you.' So, she wrote a letter and sent a photo, and one morning she says, 'I have great news. Roman Polanski wants to meet you.' We were sitting and having breakfast together, as usual. Elli would always have grapefruit and black coffee for breakfast, and I remember looking up and saying, 'I love you, Elli.'

Roman Polanski invited me to join him at the Festival dei Due Mondi (Festival of 2 Worlds), in Spoleto. I flew to Rome where Roman picked me up in his red Maserati. We drove straight from Rome to the festival. Spoleto is very beautiful; no pictures can describe it. The festival was held in an old Roman amphitheatre and the memories will stay with me forever. I've got photos with Polanski and other directors and movie stars from all over the world; the who's who of stars were all there.

At the time, Roman Polanski was directing a musical, for the first time, called *Rigoletto*. He was well-known, of course, for his movies, but this was his first time directing a stage production. It was quite a magical experience. We stayed in one of Roman's beautiful houses, one of the many houses he had. One moment I remember was having breakfast and Roman saying, 'would you like scrambled egg?' He said it in Polish, which brought back memories of home for me; Roman being Polish too. There were always people coming and going from Roman's house. One day I picked up a newspaper and saw the story of his murdered wife, Sharon Tate, on the first page. I won't go into the story here, you can research it if you wish, but although this was 1974 and the murder had happened in 1969, it was still very close and I felt a little weird, with the media still mentioning it whenever stories of Roman appeared in the papers. The timing was a little off, for anything to happen romantically with us, if you know what I mean. But, of course, with my new-found fame in Germany, the newspapers were going crazy, announcing that we were engaged.

Hello Darlink!

I spent a beautiful time with Roman Polanski and his people in his stunning house in Rome, on Via Appia Antica. Then I had to fly back to Munich for one of my movie shoots.

Roman was away directing Chinatown when he next invited me back to Italy. He wasn't even there when I arrived, I was just invited to stay. So, I got a taxi and told the driver the address, which I still remember today. It's funny the things that stand out in our memory. I specifically remember the taxi trip, because the driver tried to cheat me out of half-a-million lira, a fair amount of money at the time! You have to be very careful in Italy when you're travelling, and of course all over the world, as many people will try and cheat you…but the difference in Italy is they do it with such charm you almost don't mind. But I guess I did mind, as this event sits so firmly in my memory.

At the end of my time in Rome, I was introduced to Omar Sharif. More of that to come!

Movie poster for La fiancée qui venait du froid

Chapter 8
VIENNA – PARIS

When I returned to live in Vienna for the second time, I ended up staying for 2 years. It was because I decided I wanted to have a 'normal' job – whatever that means! I got a position as the PR manager at the Vienna Hilton. With my incredible energy, I was in charge of liaising with huge international stars, some of them I knew personally. I would organise their stay in Vienna, dealing with publicity and the media, arranging their social schedule and more. Well remembered are Sammy Davis Jr. and Gunter Sachs, as well as people and friends I had encountered living in other countries, from other chapters of my life and throughout my career.

Unfortunately, I had a lot of corporate envy. I learned the hard way what the corporate world can be about. To me, it seems it has nothing to do with loyalty or commitment to the job; everybody wants to better themselves and when an opportunity comes along, they just move on. The small exposure I had to corporate life left me with a very sour taste.

One day, whilst living in Vienna I received a phone call from a famous Austrian film-maker, Franz Antel. I had already acted before in two of his movies. He was a very established, senior movie producer, and at that time, he was famous for doing special 'Friday dinners' in Vienna. It was always exciting to be invited to his dinner parties. They were in his huge house with a long table of about 25 people. As a starter, he would serve 3 kilo boxes of Russian caviar, having them delivered directly from Russia, by train.

He was a very good and passionate cook. I still remember the taste of his beef stroganoff today. He was also a very passionate lover of women. He was married about four times. Without judgement, his wives were on average 30 years younger than him, so he was a movie story himself. He called me one day and says, 'Barbara, are you coming for Friday dinner?' I told him I already had dinner arranged, but he added, 'we also have a French director visiting Vienna and he's looking for a leading actress in his autobiography movie which he'll be shooting soon in Paris. He saw your picture in *The Actress Guide* and he's very interested in speaking with you. So, are you ok to come on Friday?'

I arrived at his house, along with about another ten actors and actresses from Vienna. The French director, Charles Nemes, was there looking the epitome of a French director. If I were to draw a French cartoon, it would look the same as Charles that night. He was wearing checked trousers, and a striped shirt. Nothing matched. His hair was shaggy and he wore round glasses.

He was so very passionate about his story, he almost glowed in the dark. He told the story in English and German, and as I'm hearing the story, I'm thinking, *oh, my God, if I don't get this part, I die. Nobody can do the part like me.* Bear in mind, my last movie had been Hajka, almost 4 years before.

This was his own life story; the story of a Polish girl he was asked to marry. She was working as a Solidarity supporter in Poland, having been to jail before because of her campaigns against the government. And she would go to jail again if she didn't leave the country.

She just needed a green card and to get out of Poland. A friend asked Charles if he would marry her, 'just for a little while!' They marry and he falls in love with her, but she moves on.

Her name was Zosia and she, of course, was Polish. The director doesn't know I'm Polish as he found me in The Actress Guide as Barbara Nielsen, under my acting name. He looked at me saying, 'do you speak French?' 'Un peu,' I replied, but that was literally all the French I knew. He says, 'Okay. Fantastic. Because we're having screen tests on Tuesday, and everybody will receive a five-page script. We're going to record the casting, and I'll return to Paris. But within ten days, we're going to know who got which part, and the leading parts, *d'accord*?'

I got the script. I went home from the Friday dinner staring at the French writing I don't understand. *Mon Dieu. What am I going to do?* The screen test is on Tuesday. But I have an idea.

So, cutting it very short, on Monday lunchtime I turn up at one of the French schools in Vienna, in the hope I can get one of the students to help me. I arrived at 12.45pm during lunch break in my Golf convertible. I had my Cabriole top down and they all came out.

I said, 'Guys, which one of you speaks the best French?' They laugh and say Andrew. Andrew is 13. I say, 'Andrew, I need your help urgently. I'm an actress and I want to get a part in a French movie. I need the script translated from French to German, and then I can learn the French phonetically. Will you help me?' He agrees, so I say 'great! Let's call your mum.'

I was so lucky… I think his mum wanted the afternoon off! I introduced myself, gave her my ID number and offered to buy them both lunch. I didn't want to say dinner, but as it was, we had to have dinner too.

He went home at 8.30pm that night. We were sitting and recording the French words into a little tape recorder. I was speaking French phonetically. He says, 'you're going to get the part.' By then, I did believe I would get the part.

I did the screen test, and within six days, I got a message from Paris to say, 'You got the leading part. We want you in Paris in the next week or so to do publicity, meet the crew, do all the promos. Then you can return to Vienna and get everything in order before coming back to Paris for the actual shoot.'

Another chapter of my life began in that moment.

Publicity for La Fiancée qui venait du froid
(The Bride Who Came in From The Cold)

Chapter 9

ARRIVING IN PARIS – FRENCH CONNECTION

Even before I had the privilege of working in French movies, you could show me excerpts of movies without sound, without names, and I could guess which one was the French movie. I would know because they have a different pace; incredibly slow and real. And it's astounding because the French people actually live their lives 'fast'. They speak fast and move fast, like they don't want to miss anything. They constantly have a fear of missing out. Obviously, Paris, is a mecca of cinema. And in the mid-80s French people loved movies. They would go to the cinema and stand in a queue to socialise before going in to see the movie. I once stood in a queue behind Catherine Deneuve.

When I arrived in Paris to meet the crew to do the promotional campaigns for *The Fiancee Who Came In From The Cold*, we all met in a big restaurant in Saint Germain de Pres. I'll remember that lunch forever. Going to the bathroom, there was

Hello Darlink!

a big sign, Attention a la Marche which means *be careful of the steps*. Don't worry - I didn't break anything, but I came back to the table rubbing my knee and said, 'Guys. I just learnt my first French sentence ... Attention a la Marche.

Before we started the shoot and production of the movie, I was advised, rightly so, to find a French agent. I went to the three leading agencies in Paris explaining about my lead role in the movie which was scheduled to open in 400 cinemas on the 21 September. Coincidentally, 21 September, happens to be my birthday.

All three agents said they would take me onto their books. It was a nice problem to have, but I didn't know who to choose. I went back to the hotel to call my long-standing family friend, Artur Brauner; famous German movie producer based in Berlin. I say, 'Artur, what do I do?' He told me Myriam Bru was the best, so I went with her. Myriam was a very established talent agent in France, and a former actress, married to Horst Buchholz. So now I have a French agent and a leading part in a French movie, and it doesn't seem to matter that I don't speak French! In fact, I actually needed to have a Polish accent in my new part, so of course it was meant to be.

After the promotional tour, I went back to Vienna to get my affairs in order before I had to return to Paris for the film shoot. My absolute, immediate, spontaneous conclusion was, *I'm moving to Paris*. Luckily, nothing was holding me back. I didn't have husband or children, at the time.

I quit my job in the corporate world, which I wasn't enjoying anyway, before even working out the logistics of a big move. I had no place to live and very little money. The big money from the movie wasn't due until much later. I knew a young guy, a handyman, who often helped me, and we put everything in a container to take to Paris. Within five days, I was on my way; I didn't even have time to do my washing and took my full laundry basket with me.

Crossing the Austrian-French border, I didn't yet have a work permit. The contract for the movie was signed, but the permit was still on the way. The officials asked if I was going to France for work, to which I replied, 'No, I'm going on holidays…' 'With your own laundry basket?' they said. Fair question I suppose, but I muddled through with a smile asking something like, 'would you trust a hotel with your laundry?' Somehow, I got away with it!

My experience of living in Paris started with my first French movie. Charles Nemes the director of the movie, basically translated his life story into very well-written script. My acting partner was the very famous, handsome French movie star, Thierry Lhermitte. He was already extremely well known in France, and by then he'd made many successful French movies.

A little about the movie: Thierry played an advertising agency owner who created publicity campaigns with all the beautiful people in France. His Russian ex-girlfriend, now just his friend, calls him and says, 'You have to save my best friend. Her name is Zosia, and she lives in Warsaw. She campaigns for Solidarity and she's in trouble. They've already stuck her in jail once and now she will go back if she doesn't get out of Poland. You have to marry her.' (Because Poland was communist at the time.) Well, our main character doesn't want to get married; he has never wanted to be married, especially to someone he hasn't met. But his friend convinces him; 'You believe in a good world. It's not a real marriage, it's just to help Zosia so she can be free and live outside of Poland.' After seeing her photo, he agrees and goes to meet her in Warsaw.

Ironically, all the scenes that were supposed to be in Warsaw, we shot in Vienna – the city I had just left – because Poland was still under communist rule until 1989, and we were unable to shoot the movie there.

In the movie, I pick him up in my little Polish Fiat and we drive to my little flat. Recording the scene, he says to me, 'So, Zosia, we're going to get married tomorrow for your passport to leave Poland. How long do we have to stay married?' I'm supposed to answer in French that we're going to stay married for between six months and two years; whatever is the minimum time for me to get my French passport,

In French, *deux* means two, but *douze* means twelve. So, Barbara has her speaking coach for the movie, but maybe the coach didn't work hard enough, or Barbara didn't work hard enough with the coach. He stands with his back to me, looking out of the window, saying, 'Alors, Zosia. We're going to be married tomorrow. Combien de temps? How long are we going to stay married? And I say, without even thinking, between six months and twelve years! Entre six mois et douze ans. And he turns and says in shock.

'Douze Ans?'

Therry didn't have to act, he was shocked when he turned to ask me : Deux I replied again, 'Oui, douze ans.' The crew was on the floor; the director and everybody was laughing at my pronunciation. It became a theme throughout the whole movie. When we were shooting the scene where he drives me from Warsaw to Paris, I cry all the time because I'm leaving my family behind, my beautiful Polish family. He doesn't know how to change the conversation because I've used two boxes of tissues, but he says, 'Zosia, tell me, how long were you in jail for?' He's working on building the scene to say, 'now you won't ever go back again.' And I say, 'two and a half years,' which of course, comes out as 'twelve and a half.' I am only 24 years old in the part. And the story continues…..

I experienced for the first time the joy of working in the French movie world, which is so different to any other country; it's unbelievable. The French 'joie de vivre' translates to how they work, and how they work is as follows:

As a leading actor, you receive your daily run sheet and have a choice if you want to have your makeup call before or after 11.30am. To compare, in Germany, they take you to the makeup call at about 06:00am, sometimes 4.30am if it's an early start.

The French movie day, for the actors, starts with lunch. They then proceed to shoot exactly the same number of hours, without rushing. They produce the same amount of rushes (a term used to describe what's been filmed on any given day), as in other countries that I acted in all over Europe. Most productions start shooting at 08:00 in the morning and by 1pm the makeup is falling off; you have to have it done all over again. Not so in France!

The French culture of loving life is incredible. It can be infectious and in effect, can feel too good to be true.

Every day, we had a catering company on set, which, if we were shooting outside a restaurant in San Tropez, for example, would cater a three-course lunch, with cheese and a bottle of wine. They eat slowly and they talk about life. In fact, eating is the only thing the French do slowly.

Living in Paris taught me that French people don't get fat. They eat all the things we are now told are bad for you. But it's not bad if you eat it in certain proportions, with pace and quality. Everybody has a baguette, everybody eats cheese, but there were very few overweight French people in my experience. They eat food in a way that nourishes them and gives them joy. I'm not saying the world hasn't changed, of course there will be overweight people in France, but it's a different philosophy of life. It's beautiful.

And of course, everybody drinks plenty of wine, but you don't see people binge drinking. Even though I went out a lot in Paris, I don't think I ever saw overly-drunk French people. I went to some of the most celebrated clubs and restaurants and feel so privileged to have had this life…..which brings me back to Omar Sharif!

Photographed by Jean-Daniel Lorieux

Chapter 10
OMAR SHARIF

I met Omar Sharif when I was in Rome one time and later in Paris when I was shooting *The Bride Who Came In From The Cold*. Omar invited me to the *Regine*, the very famous club in Paris. We spent all night dancing until the early morning and the Regine owner came to me and said, 'This is amazing, what have you done to him? Omar Sharif never dances.' We went for breakfast with some incredible people, and then I stayed in his beautiful villa, and was introduced to his son, Tarek. I had such an amazing time, and it was two days later when I realised I didn't have my fur coat. In those days, everyone had a fur coat! I remember calling Regine, and luckily, they had it.

So, Omar Sharif actually proposed me to marry him. He would say, 'Barbara, we're going to live on an island away from everything that is Paris, and we'll have a beautiful baby daughter.' I was invited to fly to Cannes Film festival with Omar and spend time with him in Monte Carlo, thinking I would be married to him soon after. I went to a fantastic little boutique in Munich and bought myself a most beautiful dress. It was a long white dress, not obviously a wedding dress, but I was thinking, 'this will be for Monte Carlo.' I also bought an amazing red dress, and another in gold. The boutique owner was asking lots of questions; 'What are you buying this for? Where are you going?' But I didn't tell her. I have one policy in my life; I don't say anything to anybody until something *actually* happens; until it's signed, sealed and delivered.

You learn the hard way, especially as an actor, that you don't put it out there until it's yours, so I didn't tell her I was going to Monte Carlo with Omar, and we'd be spending time with Roman Polanski. The only person who knew about Omar was my mum, because she was always my very best friend.

Omar and I would speak on the phone every night. Well, maybe night is not the right word, because his lifestyle was so different to mine. Unfortunately, he was completely addicted to gambling, not even love could crush it. When I stayed at his place for a while, I discovered he would gamble through the night, and not come home until about two in the afternoon. He would eat and then sleep until midnight before going and gambling again. Once, when he was gambling, he told me he'd lost a house that he'd bought and never even seen. And finally, Omar says to me, 'Barbara, I love you, but I cannot do it to you. I cannot make you part of my life that is not normal. It just wouldn't be fair to you.' I was heartbroken. I didn't want to understand his motivation.

Literally, a week later, I got a part in a great TV series and flew to Majorca to shoot for three months.

Every time certain music played, reminding me of Omar, I would cry so hard, and everyone could see my tears. A wonderful and famous German actress, Agnes Windeck, who played another character in the series, said, 'Who is it that makes you cry? He must be gorgeous, and he must be an idiot!' I really didn't want to tell people who it was, at the time. She continued, 'he must be an idiot, because I would be the proudest woman in the world to have a daughter-in-law like yourself.' I remember the compliment and thinking that 'not marrying' Omar was maybe a blessing in disguise. How would my life be with someone like Omar Sharif?

Obviously, in those days, he was a most beautiful man, never mind what a big star he was. With his background and where he was from, he had so much intensity. He was about living in the moment, and when he believed in something, he just did it.

I had a sliding door moment about six months later. I had finished filming in Majorca and happened to be in Munich. With some spare time, I really couldn't decide whether to turn left or right. I ended up going left, and literally, bumped into Omar, who happened to be in Munich for a couple of days.

I think it was meant to be, as we had a very lovely dinner, and a very lovely closure to our relationship, which wouldn't have happened otherwise.

I never cried over Omar again.

On the movie set in Paris Airport

Chapter 11
PARIS – PART 2

Back on the movie set of *La Fiancee Qui Venait du Froid*, the crew would speak French very, very fast. In fact, nobody in France speaks slowly. The crew think fast, live fast and talk fast. They would chat away with me, and I'd have to say, 'Sorry. Please slow down. I don't speak French.'

I remember them looking at me sideways; 'of course you speak French.' I had to explain, I could only speak what was in my script. I made a resolution to go to Alliance Francaise to learn to speak French properly. In the meantime, George Glass, the French producer of the movie, suggested I watch TV in French and one day I will understand it all.

I didn't understand much at first, but one day it just happened. I watched the French news, and I understood it. I was so excited, I picked up the phone and called George. 'I understood all the news,' I told him!

Alliance Francaise had a most unique learning system. We were not allowed to speak any word other than French; not the teacher, not the pupils, nobody. The teachers showed us images and talked to us, and we would reply in French.

By then, I already spoke four languages, so whoever needed something translated into English, Russian, German or Polish, they were coming to me. Every time I spoke another language, they sent me out of the class. I had to sit on a yellow bench in the corridor like a naughty schoolgirl!

I did finally learn to speak fluent French when living in Paris, watching French movies, the news and other programmes. I lived in Paris for two and a half years. Deux ans et demi. And I would recommend it to everyone.

Life on the streets of Paris is incredible. Paris back then was maybe 12 million people, and I would say if 6 million were asleep, the other 6 were on the streets restaurants, shops cafes, cinemas. They don't go home. They love to celebrate life. I would sit in a cafe and watch the best performance theatre in the world – the streets of Paris.

The way people dress and move. Their love of life …. and shopping. Everyone is carrying something, while they walk their dog! Everybody has a dog. And the dogs very often look like the owners, or the owners look like their dogs.

I remember sitting in one of the finest restaurants in Paris, Brasserie Lipp, which is still very celebrated today. Jean Paul Belmondo was sitting across from me, staring at me, and I was staring at him because he was so famous. Next to me, was a couple drinking the most expensive champagne with a huge dog at the table sniffing at the pate foie gras. And it was all okay.

The French people would go out to restaurants at 10.30 at night. I remember a conversation with a French couple who said, 'oh, we actually have sex before we go for dinner, so we don't have to worry about it later.' I asked one of the French guys, as a joke, 'Guys, you talk about sex all the time. Are you all so slim because you have so much sex?' They said, 'No, it's because we run so much to get it.'

I regularly remember being in Castel nightclub at 2am in the morning and people going off to another venue. But they're all professional people, not people who lie in bed all day. I wondered how they did it.

One guy said, 'I actually don't feel tired because the adrenaline is still pumping. When you enjoy your night, you enjoy your day. And if you're tired the next day, you have an early night, and then you do it all over again.'

While living in France, I made another three feature movies. I was always cast as a foreign woman, because of my accent, and working in French movies was magic. But working in showbiz there's always murphy's law. There's either nothing coming in, or you get two movies at the same time, and you have to say 'no' to one of them. However, while in Paris, this wasn't the case. I got cast for another movie called *Tranches De Vie* (Slices of Life) also written by Francois Leterrier, celebrated writer and director. The movie was eleven episodes of self-standing stories with another very big French star, Gerard Jugnot, who had worked with me in the previous movie. I played a Russian woman from the country, and we go back in time.

This movie was shot at the same time as *L'année des méduses* (Year of the Jellyfish) since we were shooting *Tranches De Vie* at night and this one during the day. That's why I could do both. Never mind my adrenaline, I was exhausted. I was so tired I remember when we were shooting at the airport, and I was sitting on a bench dressed as a Russian woman in a scarf, country clothes, with makeup for no makeup. The crew had just moved on from the airport without me, while I was sat on the bench having fallen asleep. The French cops came and asked if I was ok! I was asking if they knew where my crew was, but they had no idea what I was talking about!

I was very excited to be cast in the movie *L'année des méduses*, based on the book written by Christopher Frank. I had watched his movies for years, always thinking, *I wish I could meet this guy*. He was an iconic French director and screenwriter.

His movies were always about women, and I often wondered; *how does he understand women's pain? How can he tap into our emotions? How can a man do that? I'm dying to meet him one day.*

One day, on coming home to my flat, I played my answering machine to see if there was any good news, and I hear, 'Barbara, this is your agent, Myriam Bru. Christopher Frank is casting parts for a movie which will be called *The Year of the Jellyfish* shot in St Tropez. They'd like to see you for the casting tomorrow.'

Tomorrow. Christopher Frank. *Oh, my God.* I walked into the production company the next day and already on the wall was a picture of Valerie Kaprisky with the leading role. She was extremely famous then as she'd acted in a movie with Richard Gere called *Breathless*.

So, she was the lead. I was being cast as a German character called Barbara. Next to Valerie's picture on the wall, was my photo too which they had got from the agency, with the screen test scheduled for the following day. Now comes the most amazing story.

I'm told that they will confirm, in maybe four weeks, who is going to get the parts…and that's showbiz. *Don't call us, we'll call you.* So, you can be dying inside from not knowing, but you can't call them. At the time, I was flying from Paris to South Africa because I was visiting my 'new love interest'. Douglas and I met on a blind date in Paris, and we're still married today. When we first met, he would come to Paris from South Africa, almost every weekend.

One day he says, 'I'd love you to come to Johannesburg. to see what I do and where I live.' At that time, I didn't know I was going to marry him, but the relationship was going at quite a speedy pace. I arrived, in Johannesburg, and stayed in his beautiful Penthouse apartment for about seven days. One morning, we were sitting having a delicious croissant for breakfast, and drinking coffee. His secretary from his office upstairs, calls and says, 'Excuse me, we've received a telegram for Barbara Nielsen.'

I open it and the telegram says, 'Congratulations. You have won the part in *L'année des méduses.* We need you back in Paris to be in St Tropez next week.' I put the telegram down, looking directly at Douglas, my future husband, and said, 'Darlink, I'm so sorry, I have to go.'

It was the best thing that ever happened. I had to go to St Tropez for three months with a bunch of big French stars, including Caroline Cellier and Bernard Giraudeau. The movie was a very slow-paced thriller, and Valerie Kaprisky played a very naughty, seductive young girl. She has an affair with an older man. Well, everybody has affairs in France. And then the intrigue comes as I, German tourist Barbara, become her lesbian affair. Never mind, we are all married. That is French cinema. Almost

French reality in a way. The French treasure love and joy and obviously, you can't generalise, but it's very common. And St Tropez was quite an experience as well, because, of course, it's amazing, and beautiful. The production had organised exclusive access to a portion of the beach, just for our recording for three months.

I was introduced to French director, Screenwriter, Roger Vadim, and met some incredible people. Douglas, my then boyfriend from Johannesburg, came to visit because he was missing me terribly. He was always the most generous man, spoiling me like a princess. He arrived to the beautiful resort where the crew were staying, and showered me with presents. He bought me beautiful jewellery; a Cartier watch and an antique Victorian butterfly brooch that when you separated it, turned into two earrings. He had it all locked in his suitcase.

We both went out for a jog, as I was very sporty and loved running … I still do my walking almost daily today.

2 hours later we're back in the room. I'm in the shower getting ready to go for dinner and I hear Douglas saying, 'Barbara, darling. Would you like to wear your Cartier watch, or any jewellery?' 'Sure, I'll wear the watch,' I say, and then I hear, 'Oh shit! The suitcase is broken. We've been robbed.' Someone had broken in and taken everything.

They took all the jewellery, as well as a lot of cash he had with him; watches, jewellery, everything. As we sat by the pool, we called the police and I remember saying to Douglas, 'What's the time?' He laughed and said, 'Are you kidding? We don't have any watches.'

This was before smart phones of course.

But what was disappointing was that when the cops arrived, they were not interested in our situation at all. We thought perhaps they were in on the conspiracy. 'Give us proof,' they said. 'What about receipts?' Douglas was shellshocked. 'Look,' he said. 'I mean, the key is broken, the suitcase is broken. Can you at least take a fingerprint?' But they did not.

So, there's another side to France. There's another side to every country. Of course, it's not paradise, but it could be as close as it gets. Never mind, it's just possessions. We still had a beautiful time.

I had a similar experience living in my apartment in Paris, two days before I left for my wedding in Johannesburg, I had all my gifts prepared that I had bought to take for people there. I told the concierge I was leaving to go to South Africa to get married, so the apartment would be closed up for a while. Coming back from a little shopping, I discovered my apartment broken into; everything on the floor, everything gone.

Except for my beautiful mink coat. It was hanging at the back of a cupboard and somehow, they didn't see it. It's a horrible experience to feel so violated. It wasn't just that the possessions, travel cheques and all the gifts were gone, it was the feeling of somebody invading my place, like I was no longer safe.

So why did I leave my life in beautiful, vibrant Paris? My prince on a white horse from Johannesburg asked me to marry him.

Style Magazine cover with Douglas

Douglas and me in Paris

At a fashion event in Perth

Chapter 12
DOUGLAS – A LOVE STORY!

I want to apologise for not talking about all my husbands. I have been married several times. As a young woman, I didn't know how to say 'No' and almost anyone who asked me to marry them, I said, 'yes.' But I *will* talk about Douglas, my last husband, as we have now been married for almost 40 years.

Not to be critical of Valentines Day but we never celebrate that day; we celebrate our love every day. I remember a time during our early days when Douglas bought me a beautiful HUGE bunch of flowers. He said, 'I'll bring you flowers for all your life!' I think manifesting love is something to be done 365 days of the year. Love is about lots of laughing and doing special things for each other every day.

I was living in Vienna, for the second time, when I was first heard about Douglas. Living in a maisonette flat in a beautiful district in Vienna, the building had a sauna and swimming pool downstairs, and it was painted in a beautiful sunny yellow colour. It was a wonderful place to live. I met a young Polish girl there called Lydia who lived in my block of apartments.

One day Lydia was telling me about her friend, Fritz, who lived in South Africa. They had a long-distance relationship. He was very handsome, and she liked him very much. They would spend hours talking on the phone, but she wasn't sure about the relationship, because he was living so far away. One day Lydia excitedly says, 'Fritz is coming to visit me here in Vienna.' When Fritz arrived, Lydia wanted me to meet him. It's funny what we women remember. She called me and said, 'you have to come now,' and I remember I was wearing a red and white dress; half white, half red, Polish colours obviously, and high heels. Fritz was a very handsome, sophisticated man, originally from Austria. As Lydia introduced me, I say, 'Hi, I'm Barbara.' And Fritz says, 'Wow! I think you have to meet my friend, Douglas.' I then asked, without any prejudice; 'What colour is he?' Hello – that would be on the news today. He just started laughing and said, 'he's Scottish. I'm Austrian and he's Scottish.' And they both lived in Johannesburg, South Africa. We had dinner a few times during his visit, but Douglas was not mentioned again.

Some months later I moved to Paris. One day, Lydia informed me that she and Fritz were going skiing in Switzerland, and they would come to Paris to visit as part of the trip. Douglas, the friend Fritz had mentioned, was also travelling with them. I found out later they were coming to Paris so that Fritz could propose to Lydia to marry him. So, I had never met Douglas until he phoned me one day and asked me to go for dinner with him, on a blind date.

Hello Darlink!

I met Douglas, Fritz and Lydia at the famous Ritz Hotel, as Douglas was staying there. We were to go on to Maxims for our first date. He was pretty gorgeous and as he took my coat from my shoulders, he said with a very sexy voice, 'where would you like to get married one day?' I looked at him sideways, saying, 'I'm not planning on getting married for quite a while. I'm having an amazing time here in Paris, living my life and being free.' It was fun and it was the truth.

Our first date in Paris was very special. Paris was vibrant in those days and Maxims was pumping, full to the last table and chair. We had such a good time; I remember I ordered a beautiful French fish dish - but I didn't touch my food. The Maître D came over about three times to ask if something was wrong with the food. 'Nothing's wrong,' I said, 'we're just having such a great time, I forgot to eat.' There was a band playing that night, and a long table across from us with people from Saudi Arabia; one of whom was a Saudi prince, about 14 years old. One of the guys from his table came and asked me to dance, to which I said, 'okay, but only if my table dances with us.' At that point all the security guards jumped up from their table, protecting the young prince. In the end, the 14-year-old boy paid for the whole table.

The next day, Douglas and I went for another beautiful dinner. And the next day we went for a delicious lunch. And it continued. When he had to fly back to South Africa, he would send me recorded messages singing the most beautiful songs. After a while, he would fly from Johannesburg to Paris almost every weekend. I think it was about an 11-hour flight, which I'm sure was exhausting to come so regularly, especially when you have your own business to run.

But, of course, my life was busy, and it was the time of year when my mum visited. Everywhere I lived in the world, whether I lived in a small apartment or a big apartment, if I lived alone or with somebody in my life, my mum would always come and stay with me for three months. She was the most well-travelled mum in Poland!

So, my mum was coming to Paris, and I told her she was going to meet Douglas. We went to meet him at the Ritz Hotel, which was where he always stayed. He came out in a beautiful cape, looking like a prince. My mum hadn't met him yet but she whispered, 'that's him. He's the one.' The three of us went out that night to a beautiful club called Alcazar; a very exclusive restaurant and night club.

This was at the time when *The Fiancee Who Came In From The Cold* had opened in 400 cinemas across France. I was in a lot of magazine features and TV interviews. The host on the stage at the club said, 'Tonight we have a special guest; Miss Barbara Nielsen.' And mistakenly, the spotlight went on my mum, not on me. It doesn't matter, my mum looked so young and so beautiful. She looked like a young Zsa Zsa Gabor. People kept sending champagne to our table that night. Between the three of us, I think we drank about nine bottles of champagne. The performance at the club later that night was Russian Ballet and Russian dancers. It was a most amazing and memorable night. This kind of magic continued for some time, while Douglas would fly away and I stayed in Paris, smelling the sheets. There were many times too, when I was filming and not available for social dates.

This carried on for about a year, and of course, we were in love by then. However, me being in the movies, I had to go out and be a social butterfly. I had to be flirty too. I wasn't doing bad things, but I had to attend all sorts of events. But Douglas was the same. I clearly remember the first time I visited him in Johannesburg. Douglas and his driver collected me in his Rolls Royce. He still had some work to do in his office, so I had some time to unpack slowly and relax. I picked up a magazine from a basket, purely by chance, and on the front cover there's Douglas with a rose in his mouth and the headline, 'too many women, too little time.'

The article said that Douglas 'breaks the hearts of so many women across Johannesburg but says he will never get married.' So, the journalist who interviewed him asked, 'and what about the actress in Paris? We've been hearing some gossip that you're in love. Would this change your decision of getting married?' And Douglas replied with something silly like his life philosophy is my life philosophy; 'Life is too beautiful not to be free,' he said.

I threw the magazine at him when he came in. 'You know what?' I said, 'next time you mention me in your interviews, please ask for permission. I'm not just an actress in Paris, I'm Barbara Nielsen who is telling you I wouldn't even consider being married to you. We're both having a beautiful time, so don't use my name amongst others you're dating while I'm not here.'

Funny looking back now, Douglas is actually a one-woman man, as I am a one-man woman. Everything he was doing then was because he was free, because he could. He told me once that he was discouraged from getting married because he had seen so many married people having external affairs. He also had a lot of married women chasing him. That does make sense. He was always thinking, *what's the point of marriage if all these people do all the things they want to do anyway?*

September came around, and it was my birthday. We took a beautiful trip from Paris to Venice on the Orient Express, and Douglas says, 'I have a surprise for you.' I was actually thinking he was going to pop the question. I felt the way we were living had been going on for too long. I had to know what I was doing with my life….if I was free. The day came when he showed me the surprise. He opened a beautiful box with another, beautiful piece of jewellery. But in that moment, I made a decision; this would be the last trip.

We arrived back in Paris and I suggested, 'Darlink, let's go to Brasserie Lipp to have a drink. There's something I want to tell you.'

We sat and ordered a drink and I said to him, 'look, I love you, you love me. We 've had a year of beautiful romance and wonderful times but I have a problem. I live in Paris; you live in Johannesburg. Obviously, it's far away. You arrive like a prince on a white horse and then you leave. I smell the sheets and look at my jewellery and my photos and I'm actually disabled from living my life. So, I'm so sorry but I want you to go back to Johannesburg. I booked your flight tonight at 9.45pm.'

I wasn't acting, I meant every word. Douglas stared at me saying, 'oh, tonight?' 'Yeah,' I said, 'I have things to do, I'm busy tomorrow.' He replied, 'Ok then. But before I pack, before I go, can we please stop in at Notre Dame?' I only lived ten minutes from there, so we go into the Notre Dame, and walking in he takes me to the main altar, goes down on his knees and says in front of God, 'I would love to ask you to marry me and give me a child.' And I said, 'YES'. We had a photo taken by somebody who was passing by just a few minutes later. He didn't pack or leave that night.

And soon after, we were married. For some reason, I always forget our anniversary in November. Partly, I suppose, because of the apartment break in, which happened the night before I flew to Johannesburg to get married.

Of course, the environment of living in in Paris is completely different to Johannesburg. One of my best memories of Paris was going to Brasserie Stella every Monday. I would eat Steak Tartare with a glass of champagne. It was magic. Though today I wouldn't touch Steak Tartare if you threatened to kill me! But in those days, I'd eat it with brown toast, and it was absolutely delicious. Several years later I was in Paris, (as I was frequently), and as it was Monday, I suggested to my friend that we go to Brasserie Stella, as we used to.

As we sat down, the waiter said in French, 'Hello, Barbara, we haven't seen you for a while. Is it brown toast and steak tartare as usual?'

With my children in our house in Johannesburg

Chapter 13

SOUTH AFRICA – MY BABIES

Douglas and I were married in November 1984, and I returned to Paris, to sell my car and close up my apartment. I lived in Johannesburg from 1985 to 2000, Until Perth, and apart from my childhood, it was the longest I had lived anywhere in my life!

Our wedding in Johannesburg was very low-key. The priest came to Douglas' penthouse apartment dressed in a beautiful white safari suit. Douglas contacted my parents in Warsaw and officially asked my father for permission to marry his daughter, as he is very traditional and respectful. It was organised so quickly that it was too short a time to fly my parents from Poland to Johannesburg. The reception was held in Douglas' business partner's house, with all his closest friends - a lot, I'm sure, were ex-girlfriends! It was very much the elite of Johannesburg society, and everyone came to see Barbara, Polish actress from Paris, who changed Douglas' ideas on getting married.

It was a massive change of lifestyle for me, especially during the first six months, I lived in a state of distress because Douglas had sales teams all over Africa, not just South Africa. He was basically travelling away all week and only coming back home for the weekend. Today, I might think that would be heaven, but not then!

I was given a driver, a maid and house cleaners, and I was feeling like a bird in a golden cage. Unfortunately, in Johannesburg, you can't simply just go and walk the street as you do in Warsaw, Munich, Paris, Perth and most cities throughout the world. In Johannesburg, you have to be almost always in either a shopping centre, or somewhere safe. At the time, it wasn't even that safe in the shopping centre! Because I was so new to the country, my driver was also my bodyguard. One day, I was sitting at home alone, trying to tell myself *I'm so happy, I'm so, so lucky* but I was missing Paris and my freedom. However, things slowly began to improve. I met some beautiful girlfriends and was introduced to the classiest of circles. I made some friendships that were so strong, they could never be repeated or duplicated in life. I also had a publicist helping with my career, and in a short space of time, I got a leading part in a TV drama in Johannesburg, hired by a very famous casting agent.

I certainly appreciate that Douglas understood I couldn't just give up my life. He is a very generous human being, not only with material things, but also in spirit. He has never tried to change me or stop me from doing what I wanted to do. When I got the leading part in the popular TV drama, I played a French girl alongside famous South African actor, Arnold Vosloo, who later became very celebrated in Hollywood in movies called *The Mummy* and *The Blood Diamond*. He played a terminally ill young artist who falls in love with a French girl. While we were in the middle of shooting, I got pimples on my face, and I remember feeling so angry. All of us get occasional pimples, it only proves we're human after all, but they came at the most unsuitable time. Maybe it was because I was having a cheese attack! I love cheese, but I was eating cheese for breakfast, cheese for lunch and cheese in the afternoon.

I told the makeup girl I didn't know what was happening, as I'd never had bad skin before. She said, 'any chance you might be pregnant? It looks like a pregnancy mask to me!' I was shocked, but I did a test, and YES, I was pregnant with our first child; our daughter, Kasia. So, there I was, in my first leading part in South Africa, pregnant and eating cheese five times a day. I was not able to have a close up from both sides. I said, 'Darlink, take any close ups on my left side, which is my chocolate side anyway.' Suddenly I started feeling as if I was home.

We were out driving a car when I told Douglas, and he stopped and touched me on my tummy. 'Oh my God. When I imagine there is a life starting to develop, which is you and me, it feels like a miracle.' It sounds a little cliche when I read it here, but it was a truly magic feeling. I know there are many people who can't have children, and some people choose not to have them, but it is the most amazing experience. When a child is so loved from the moment of conception and is wanted so much, it's magic and breathtakingly beautiful.

I was already pregnant on my birthday but didn't know it. Douglas was always good at spoiling me with beautiful gifts. He once put a diamond in an oyster! On my birthday, he tells me, 'I have one last surprise for you.' We were driving in the country, stopping in the middle of nowhere, and I see a beautiful black horse coming towards me. Douglas says, 'I'd like to introduce you to your horse.' Douglas had bought me a beautiful racehorse as one of my gifts. 'Can you ride?' he asked. 'Of course,' I said. I had ridden in one of my movies. I went for a quick ride on my new gift, but it wasn't long before I was on the floor, because it was such a powerful racehorse! Then four weeks later, I discovered I was pregnant, and we had to sell the horse. So that was my very short riding career.

Because I was pregnant and our little family was growing, we moved to a beautiful house in a wonderful place called Houghton Drive. The penthouse was now just the office. And soon, our beautiful daughter Kasia (pronounced Kasha) was born. We gave her a Polish name; the Polish version of Katrina. Like I'm Barbara, but the Polish version of Barbara is Basia (pronounced Basha). That's what everybody calls me. My mum was Zofia, but everybody called her Zosia. So Basia. Kasia, Zosia.

And as you do in South Africa, we had plenty of security, and in our luxurious new home, I had two maids and a gardener to run our beautiful garden. We also had a driver who arrived every morning to take Douglas to work. And when I came out of hospital with Kasia , I also had a night nurse.

When Kasia was about three years old, I got a part in a movie co-production about the life of Albert Schweitzer. The cast included very prestigious actors Susan Strasberg and Malcolm McDowell, from A Clockwork Orange. I was cast for the part as a nurse who was a real character in Albert Schweizer's life. Her name was Rachel and she became his right-hand assistant. His wife was very jealous of her. The movie was shot in Natal, near Durban.

It was an international co-production, with a set built to look like the village where Albert Schweitzer lived. Shooting the movie, we would leave the hotel for the location at 04:00 in the morning. We had our makeup and costumes done to start shooting by 8.30am. We were completely cut off from the outside world. After a few weeks, I realised I was late with my period. But it seemed that many of the girls were in the same situation. Susan said it was the change in climate and the hectic schedule. I read a book on reflexology, and it said if you are late with your period, you can put a teaspoon and press on your tongue until you feel sick - then you should get your period within two to three days.

This actually worked for most of the girls, but not for me. So, after four weeks, Susan says, 'Why don't you have a blood test done when you get back to Durban?' I did the blood test but couldn't get the results as we were busy shooting every day and I didn't have time. Ironically, we were filming a scene delivering twin babies. One of the characters in the movie is an African lady giving birth to twins. We had a real doctor, of course, on set, showing us nurses the correct instruments and what to do during a delivery. It was the most chaotic scene, as we went through about six sets of twins because the twins were crying or there was no continuity, or the twins were too tired or too big.

My assistant had been in Durban, and I had given her authority to pick up my results. When we finally finished shooting the scene, she handed me the envelope with the results, but I was exhausted and unsure what they meant. I tapped the on-set doctor on his shoulder and said, 'I'm so sorry, Doctor, please refresh my memory: but how can I tell if I'm pregnant.' 'Positive or negative?' he says, 'which one have you got?' 'Positive,' I said. 'Well congratulations, you're pregnant.' So again, I found out I was pregnant with my son, on the set of a movie.

When Douglas came to visit me on the weekend, I was waiting at the airport and as he arrived I said, 'I have an amazing surprise for you.'

Douglas replied with a smile, 'I know. You're pregnant and he's going to be a boy.' *Wow, how did he know that?* 'We're going to call him Oscar,' I said, 'because if I don't get an oscar for this movie, then he will be my Oscar.' Every time I have a baby, I find out I'm pregnant on a movie set! But Oscar was named Jay because Douglas had the choice of our boy's name, as I had chosen our girl's name. My beautiful babies; Kasia and Jay.

My Albert Schweitzer movie was an incredible experience. Working with the best actors in the world, they don't act. They become the part, the character, and they put their own intuition into the story. When you're transported into a different era, even the lines come easily. It becomes a part of you. It's effortless.

Africa is a most beautiful continent and South Africa is a wonderful country. The people are beautiful; happy, community-spirited and enjoying life. Thinking today about how we lived in South Africa it seems like another world. It was normal there for certain groups of people, to have an extremely abundant and luxurious lifestyle, but then there were people living a very different life. Most of the locals don't envy you, they actually don't want your lifestyle. *We* think they would like our lifestyle, but they have different values, different beliefs and aspirations. That's where I first became aware we have to understand, acknowledge and respect different cultures and not try to force our views, our habits or our way of living on others, even if we believe we're doing it to help them.

That's a big message, right? It's important to realise that just because we think and aspire to something for ourselves, it doesn't mean it will suit somebody else. We're here to guide, not to control. I believe this goes for our children too. Even with the knowledge I have today, I don't think I would have done things differently. I have always given my children a lot of freedom and I'm extremely grateful to my parents for the freedom they gave me.

With Malcolm McDowell on a movie set

South African Newspaper Article.

Chapter 14
SOUTH AFRICA – NEW LIFE

The last movie I made while I lived in Paris, *L'année des méduses,* was released on the circuit in France when I was already living in Johannesburg, so I hadn't seen the movie. But one day, I discovered a French Film Festival was being promoted at a cinema in Norwood; a popular suburb in Johannesburg, and my movie was showing on the programme.

Because the movie happens in Saint Tropez on the beach where most of the characters are topless, I thought perhaps I would hate it. Douglas was away, so I decided to go see the movie by myself, putting my hair in a ponytail and wearing sunglasses, so no-one could recognise me! It was actually a pretty cool movie and I loved it. Surprisingly, walking out of the cinema people were coming up to me saying, 'Barbara, can we have your autograph?' My character in the movie was also called Barbara! How did they recognise me? Obviously, my disguise didn't work. I decided to introduce myself to the cinema owner … it was some kind of gut instinct. I thought if I walked in and told him who

I was, it would be like I just stepped down from the screen. His name was Len Davies, and we became great friends. It feels like it was meant to be that I met him. I could have just gone home!

Len introduced me to an incredible woman who was organising the French Film festival. Ivana was involved in organising multiple culture festivals all over South Africa. She was a very vivacious Jewish woman with big black hair and incredible energy. I was impressed with her life and started to feel guilty that I wasn't fulfilled in my own. I mean, I was mother to beautiful children, living in a luxurious home with a wonderful husband, not wanting for anything,

But I was missing being creative, I badly needed a project. I was reminded of the time I went to see a Sangoma; a magical Zulu woman (what we might call *a medium)*. A friend had gifted me her appointment, and I remember walking into a big room which had the most incredible energy. I can't remember all the things she told me that day, but I do remember her saying, "….when you were born, the spirit of a young girl who passed away entered your body, and you will always be young. You have a young spirit guiding you."

Whether you believe in this sort of thing or not, it really made sense to me. It's why I have a youthful energy, love rap music and enjoy going to concerts. I never dress for my age! I have a true connection with young people, and rarely work with people my own age, as they just don't seem to manifest the way I do. I am not my age - I am my energy.

So, I realised something was missing, and that something, was *Barbara needed a project.* I had worked all my life, studied and created; I needed to do *more, in addition to being wife and mother.*

Ivana and I and had been friends for a long time, when one day over coffee, I said, 'Ivana, I think what you do is amazing. If there is any project I could share with you, I would love to work with you, because to be honest, from one woman to another, I feel horrible when I don't work. I don't need to work for money, but I do need to feel fulfilled. What do I talk about with my husband when I only ever go shopping or for lunch with the girls?'

One day Ivana calls me and says, 'honey, I just got a project, but I can't do it myself. I've just got too much on, with five festivals to organise. I thought it would be great for you to get involved. The National School of the Arts need to raise funds for urgent repairs.'

She continued, 'They need to rebuild. The floor is literally falling apart. I can just see you there Barbara, with all those artists and musicians! You'll rock it! We have a meeting with the board on Monday at 2.30pm. I'll introduce you, but then I have to run because I have a plane to catch to Durban.'

I turned up to the meeting and, just like that, was given the portfolio to raise funds for The National School of the Arts. They needed to raise about 20 million Rand and didn't know where to start! *How do I raise that sort of money?* I had no idea, but my entrepreneurial spirit started to kick in.

The first thing I did was to visit the father of one of my daughter's friends at school, who owned a big publishing house. I arrived at the meeting, dressed up and feeling amazing, sure he would be able to help me. I told him how The National School of the Arts was the first multi-cultural school in South Africa and how they desperately needed R20 million for building repairs. He looked me in the eye and said, 'Honestly Barbara, if we didn't know each other and I didn't know your background, I would think you were just a silly blonde, because you can't just walk into any company and ask for that sort of money. You need to have a proposal written, detailing different levels of sponsorships. You have to show the benefits they will receive in return. And you have to micromanage to get the big picture covered.' I'm glad my intuition was right and I'd chatted with him first!

For lunch one day, I met with an influential young woman, Wendy Applelbaum, whose family ran Liberty Life, a huge Insurance company. She explained and introduced me to the structure of sponsorship proposals, with different levels of benefits. I just had to write it. Her guidance helped me in raising sponsorships in the many years to come. She suggested some of the banks might be interested in supporting The National School of the Arts.

I contacted the First National Bank based in Johannesburg. After many calls and lots of rejection, from the manager and the general manager, I finally booked a meeting with the managing director. I woke up that morning with a migraine from being tense and quite nervous. It's funny, I couldn't decide what to wear that day, so I ended up with one big silver earring and one gold earring – totally not matching! I remember it was pouring with rain outside. Lucky for me, I had a driver who took me to the meeting. Because of the weather, the traffic was bad, so I pulled out my mobile phone (the size of a brick) and called Mr Miller to let him know we were stuck in traffic. He said, 'Well, I had half an hour. If you arrive in 15 minutes, we will have 15 minutes.'

Very late, I walked into his beautiful office and Mr Miller looked like a young Michael Douglas behind his desk. I began by telling him the vision for The National School of the Arts, and I was enthusiastic, because I really believed in what I was doing. I really do love the school and their mission. I loved the multiculture collaborations they had. I was able to show why they needed the funds and what they needed it for. I got my first R75,000 in sponsorship that day. Though I do remember him looking at me slightly confused….a strange accent and two completely different big earrings! The first question that comes from everyone is, 'where are you from?' Well, of course, I'm from everywhere!

I was feeling confident and successful having secured the first lot of funding, and as we were driving home I saw a sign for another Investment Bank….'stop the car!' I said. I walked in and managed to arrange a meeting with the manager. At that meeting a few days later, I got another R20,000 sponsorship.

I also managed to connect with a gentleman from De Beers, the biggest diamond mining company in the world. Mr Greenham and I had a great telephone connection, laughing and joking for about six months before we met in person. It took six months of chatting before I was able to get an appointment to follow up on the sponsorship request, I had previously emailed.

I was on holiday with my two children in Plettenberg Bay, when my brick phone rang. We were sitting having ice cream when I answered. 'Hi. This is Mr. Greenham. I've approved the appointment you wanted…. on Wednesday. Are you free?' As the call was on Monday, I had just two days to organise the two-hour flight back to Johannesburg, Lucky I was able to leave the kids for the short time I was away with their nanny and other friends we were with. I didn't hesitate; it had taken so long to get the meeting. 'Absolutely,' I said. 'Just to verify,' he continued, 'it is R165,000 you're asking for, right?' I had only previously mentioned R65,000 but of course, I agreed. 'Absolutely,' I said again. 'Great,' I think we've got it through the first door. See you Wednesday at 3.' ..... Bye guys, mummy has to fly back to Johannesburg.

The beautiful old De Beers' building was in the heart of the city, which was not ideal, because it was very dangerous in that area. I went through strict security at the reception and was sent down a long corridor for my meeting with Mr Greenham. I imagined him with lots of good energy because we'd had so much fun on the phone over the previous six months.

Walking down the corridor, I knocked on the first door. Nobody's there. Knocking on the second door, there's a lady there. Third door, nobody. It took a few doors before I found Mr Greenham, and unfortunately, we didn't laugh once. But I did get the R165,000. Along with the other sponsorship I raised, The National School of the Arts was able to refurbish the Department of Modern Music and a Media Lounge. I arranged for a plaque to be awarded to De Beers for contributing to the refurbishment,

Prior to Nelson Mandela's release from jail, the ANC were planting bombs everywhere. You could be in a shopping centre and suddenly there would be an explosion. The crime in South Africa was becoming *just too much*. We were in Cape Town when Nelson Mandela was released from jail and a large segment of the population were given promises which were not realistic. The whole energy of the country shifted in very unpredictable directions. Our golden cage was becoming smaller and smaller. The shocking statistic was that there was a hijacking or rape every

Hello Darlink!

two minutes.

We would constantly meet people and friends who were personally affected. I remember going to the hairdresser and the lady sitting next to me says, 'my brother just got shot in Cape Town. He was 41.'

I went to my acupuncturist to relieve some tension and relax, and as the lady put the needles in my body, she says, 'when you drive out Barbara, make sure you go when the gate is almost closed because yesterday my patient was hijacked there'. By this time, I was already seeing a therapist as I was having panic attacks, and carrying a brown bag to help me breathe, to help me bring my breath and my energy back when I was anxious.

I really didn't want our kids to grow up in that terrible climate. I wouldn't let them watch the news, but, of course, you can't always control what they see and hear. One day they were watching TV when there was a live news broadcast saying how a Polish couple had been shot and the lady had been raped. They found her naked on the road. Kasia was chasing me around saying, 'Mum, what is rape and why are people naked?' That's when my anxiety started building because you can't hide it from children forever.

Kasia was a very talented and advanced flute player. At the age of eleven, she played solo with the National Symphony Orchestra. One day we were driving to Pretoria for music rehearsals and our driver went straight through a red light. I voiced my concern about how we could be killed by oncoming traffic going through a red light like that. 'Madame,' he said, 'if we do stop on the red light, we might also get shot. It's just a matter of which way you want to die … and that's a reality.'

One sunny Sunday morning in Johannesburg I didn't feel as happy as I should. To help my energy I suggested we should go for Sunday lunch.

We have chosen a beautiful family restaurant we liked called Mike's Kitchen. As we arrived, Jay who was 3 years old, ran out to play on a Jumping Castle.

My heavy feeling in my gut continued through the lunch. Just before dessert I looked out of the windows over the expansive gardens and had a vision;

Two African men dressed in trench coats armed with AK 47 assault rifles were crossing in slow motion towards the restaurant. I shook my head and Douglas asked

Are you okay? Yes, I replied, but would like to go home and skip dessert. We paid and left there and then. Two men wearing trench coats were having lunch at the table directly behind us. I saw this with a glimpse of my eye before leaving but chose to ignore it.

Later that day we heard on the news that Mike's Kitchen restaurant was attacked at 3 pm (we left at 2.30pm) by two robbers who emptied the cash register, robbed the guests at gunpoint and locked everyone in the cool storage room before fleeing.

I remember this vision forever and will always trust my gut feeling .

There are more stories I could share, but I think you've got the picture on how life in South Africa was affecting us as a family. I won't share too much more, except for the moment I realised I couldn't live in South Africa any longer.

My daughter is also a very talented writer. She wrote a poem called *Mandela's Blue Eyes* and it was entered into a junior writer's competition hosted at a big resort. We were so very proud when she won the Runners-Up prize. The first prize went to a 13-year-old girl who lived in a very good area, but really there was no such thing. Her poem was about a terrible incident she experienced. In the poem, after returning home from school she calls to her parents, 'Mum? Dad?' Nobody answers. She calls to her brother, nobody answers. She goes down the corridor, opens the kitchen door and sees her family tied up and she got gang raped at gunpoint. Her poem is about how lucky she is they weren't all shot, and how thankful she was that she doesn't have AIDS. I rushed to the bathroom, unable to breathe.

I started breathing into the brown bag and put cold water on my face, thinking, *I can't do it anymore. This is insane.* People were clapping, because the poem was so beautifully written, but the reason for the poem was horrible. That very night when we got home, I said to Douglas, 'Darling, I love you with all my heart, but I can't live here anymore. I can go back to a two-bedroom apartment anywhere. I didn't grow up in a mansion. But I need to be free. I just can't do it anymore.'

And within twelve weeks, we had sold our house.

We decided to move to follow in our best friends' footsteps and I'm forever grateful to Frank and Ilona, who had already made the move to Perth from Johannesburg two years prior. They were very successful and had a fantastic life in South Africa, but realised much sooner than us, that freedom and safety for the family could be achieved, without living under a cloud of expectation that something 'bad' could happen at any moment. Douglas, being Douglas, loved South Africa. He loved the country, the people and his business, and that what he was doing, was literally changing people's lives. He was training people, giving them jobs, making inroads to cleaning up the country. But that huge vision was still a long way off, and his family's happiness was compromised.

I guess some readers at this point are going to think this is a big part of our love story; Douglas gave up everything he loved, for his family.

But life's rich journey is full of twists and turns, as well as plenty of endings and beginnings. That's just what happens in life. There are always people around us who are prepared to step out of their comfort zone and make change for a variety of reasons. They are not doing it for glory. They do *life for others* without question. My father gave up his high-ranking position for me, without me even knowing. I left behind my 'almost perfect' life in Paris to experiment with the next part of my journey. You don't have to get a reward and you don't regard it as a sacrifice. It's just another step in a new direction.

1. With Ms Gina Rinehart: Momentum Most Inspiring Woman of the Year 2016.
2. PR Ball Donation to Cancer Council WA.
3. Bottom left: John Gardner at the Pink Ribbon Ball.
4. With Douglas McNaught and Robin McClellan, US Consul General, Guest speaker IWD.
5. Barbara McNaught with Hon Kevin Rudd, 26th Prime Minister of Australia.

At the 11th Anniversary of the Pink Ribbon Ball.

Chapter 15

BELLE OF THE BALL

I had only been in Perth for a couple of years and the networking business was going well, but, as mentioned previously, I wanted to bring an unmissable event to Perth, for both women and men to enjoy.

The inaugural Pink Ribbon Ball in support of breast cancer awareness, in 2003 had 300 plus guests, which was the full capacity of the ballroom at The Sheraton Perth Hotel. We had the all the media there, and the Governor of WA at the time, Hon Ken Michael OAM, who was the patron of The Cancer Council WA.

Ken is still a dear friend, associate, Rotarian and incredible person.

The ball was very moving for me because my husband's sister, who lives in Canada, is a breast cancer survivor and used her recovery journey to create a shop in Canada with merchandise to support women with breast cancer. She and her husband were so proactive in their charity work, they were awarded an 'Order of Ontario' for outstanding dedication to the community. They flew from Canada to Perth for the inaugural Pink Ribbon Ball.

Of course, I was wearing pink on the night, I remember the day before rushing to a shop to buy some new pink underwear, but then laughing and thinking, 'it really doesn't need to be pink as nobody will see it,' but it did feel good to be wearing all pink on the night. My outfit was a sequin pink skirt with a little top and scarf, designed by my good friend Ruth Tarvydas; more about Ruth later.

The MC for the very first Pink Ribbon Ball was 6PR Radio personality, Jon Lewis. I still work very closely with Jon after many years and am very proud to call him my friend. Jon called me to the stage for my address, and as I got up from my table, I stood on my skirt. My skirt was pulled down, showing *my rear* including the new pink underwear, to the whole 300 people in the room. One of the VIP guests at our table laughed so much his wife took the flower basket in the centre of the table and crashed it on his head. He was obviously in pain.

Miss Universe, the stunning Jennifer Hawkins, lost her skirt on the catwalk not long after, and I'm glad it happened to me first, so no one could accuse me of copying her. It did get a bit of media attention though! To cut a long story short, 20 years later, I have never worn a two-piece outfit to a function again. As my mum used to say: everyone should always wear nice, fresh underwear because you never know what's going to happen.

In 2015 I met Robbie, a young man running his trendy fashion boutique near my office. I informed him about the upcoming annual Pink Ribbon Ball. He was facinated and expressed interest in attending what would be his first ball ever, "but I have nothing to wear!"

Soon after he called to ask if I could come to the boutique to advise on his outfit. When I arrived, he asked me to wait and disappeared behind the curtain. I waited for what seemed forever. Finally the curtain opened and here he was wearing a stunning pink ball gown, complete with long blond wig, make up and high heels.

What do you think? he asked. It took a moment for me to catch my breath, - STUNNING, I said.

This was my first introduction to CHRYSTAL CHANDELIER! On the night of the Pink Ribbon ball, the cheering crowd of 500 guests gave a standing ovation and voted Chrystal first prize in the Belle of the Ball competition awarded each year for the best dress on the night.

Chrystal won a prize from a cosmetic skin clinic which helped him with the first steps in the transition journey.

I clearly remember asking Robbie how young he was when he knew he was different. His reply was four years old.

In my Hello Darlink! TV interview episode called, *"When He becomes She,"* Chrystal shared his journey of the struggle to find the courage to tell his father and family members about his transition. Today, Chrystal's Facebook profile reads, transwoman.

The Pink Ribbon Ball has become a signature event in WA and celebrated its 20th anniversary in November 2023. The net profits go to breast cancer research projects through the Cancer Council WA.

We've had an incredible array of testimonial speakers over the years. My heart goes out to them because they go through an horrific journey; they truly fight to be alive. They endure the most intimidating procedures, sometimes relationship breakdowns, and so much more. They go on to turn their lives around. I am always overcome with emotion whenever they stand on stage and share their journey.

Of all the speakers over 20 years now, we have only lost one. These women are so strong. They are the ambassadors, the messengers who bring awareness that helps save so many lives.

The annual Pink Ribbon Ball has continued its important mission of creating awareness and support for Breast Cancer Research. I absolutely believe that research is the biggest key to change, and we need increased awareness to fund that research; without awareness we don't move forward.

I remember the year 2015, when Kylie Minogue was diagnosed with breast cancer. That year the ball was scheduled to be held at The Sheraton on the same night as the Telethon Ball, across the road at the Perth Convention & Exhibition Centre. Of course, the Telethon Ball is the biggest night of the year in Perth, with lots of interstate and international celebrities in town. I remember people asking how I could possibly pull off a function on the same night as hundreds of people attending the Telethon Ball. However, that year, the Pink Ribbon Ball was our biggest sold-out event, and we were even forced to change the event venue because The Sheraton couldn't provide the capacity of the guest numbers in the future.

Apparently, there was a sudden awareness that young women can get breast cancer too. People were dancing on the tables, under the tables, in the hallway. They went home with pink ribbons in their hair. The speeches were so moving, with many young women speaking out about their experiences with breast cancer. We got a lot of media coverage, and it was good to see the bookings for breast cancer checks and mammograms were fully booked, in part I hope, because we had been able to increase awareness.

When it came to all the MCs for my events, I was incredibly blessed with an array of inspiring and beautiful presenters from a number of TV networks and radio stations. One of my absolute favourites was the dazzling Charmaine Dragun from Channel Ten in Perth. Channel 10 became the media supporter of the Pink Ribbon Ball, nominating Charmaine Dragun as the host for the night. We invited Charmaine to be our host again two years later, after she had moved to Sydney. She flew back to present at the ball that year with Scott Fisher, coach of the Perth Wildcats Basketball Team.

Funny story: In the early days, I didn't know that the Wildcats were Perth's premier basketball team. One year, I was behind the scenes dressing a model in preparation for the Ball, when my young assistant runs in and says excitedly, 'Barbara, there's a call for you.' I asked her to please take a message, and she said, 'but it's the Wildcats, you have to talk to them!' 'Oh, not another animal charity,' I laughed. 'Please tell them we support breast cancer awareness….we can't support the world!" She replied, 'they are the famous Basketball Team'. The Wildcats ended up becoming a big part of breast cancer awareness and supporting the Pink Ribbon Ball. We created beautiful publicity photos with all the players wearing pink bowties and sunglasses, creating a competition to discover 'who is who' with the winner getting a ticket to the Ball.

Back to Charmaine. The second time she presented at the ball, she'd been living and working in Sydney for a while.

Charmaine was well supported by everyone at Channel Ten, but what nobody knew, was that she had been suffering with depression for years. When she arrived from Sydney, I picked her up to take her to the studio and she was shaiking like a leaf. She was always a slim, beautiful girl but I could see she had lost a lot of weight. I grabbed her hand and said, 'Charmaine, are you alright?' She replied that she'd had few tough months, but she'd be okay. She'd just come back after a big trip to her home country of Serbia, visiting family. She was engaged to a beautiful young man and was doing a job she loved; she seemed to 'have it all', but we never really know what people are going through.

The raffle that year, and major fundraising item, was Barbara's invention. Instead of a boring raffle ticket, people bought a pair of sunglasses with the pink ribbons on the side. I negotiated with Argyle Diamonds, for a real pink diamond to be put into one of the pink ribbons, and whoever bought the glasses wouldn't know who they were until the winner was announced. All the MCs and speakers were wearing the shades, especially when we were drawing the prize! Charmaine looked stunning in a beautiful pink satin gown – and sunglasses! As soon as we drew the winner, the party went crazy, but Charmaine left early.

A few days later, she emailed me from Sydney sending congratulations on the incredible night and the funds we had raised. She also wanted me to send some pics of her in the gown she wore, as she wanted to show her favourite designer.

I remember going to the office the next day and finding my assistant in tears. 'Charmaine's dead….' she said. 'She jumped at The Gap.'

It wasn't long before I got a phone call from a well-known

Perth journalist asking me if I knew about Charmaine and how she died. 'I heard it was suicide,' I said. She told me then, that if that was true, she couldn't write about it. 'We can't use the word suicide in the media,' she said. Really? It was 2007. I couldn't comprehend it.

I went to Charmaine's funeral and all I could think of was how nobody was talking about 'suicide'. She was young and beautiful, she had everything, but her illness took over. Her suicide was a result of that. I kept saying to my husband, Douglas, who has always been my sounding board, 'How can people not talk about suicide when it's happening every day? Okay, I'm going to do a ball…. I'm going to do a ball in memory of Charmaine, and I'm going to create awareness about suicide - it can't be ignored.'

After I went to the funeral, I felt crushed. I said, 'I'm sorry, I can't do it Charmaine. So sorry.' It's because my balls are filled with great positive energy. The events are designed to make people happy. I have to create an incredible, enthusiastic momentum to sell the tickets. I wasn't sure a ball about 'suicide awareness' would be the right fit.

But of course, when something is meant to be… things just happen! Within months, I was exposed to unbelievably sad events, one after another. And that was male suicide. A friend of my son took his own life on his 20th birthday. Another friend from school, aged just 16, took his life. And another friend's husband, in his 60s, took his life too.

In this time, I met a charismatic and professional music producer writing jingles; very passionate about his work. He became extremely enchanted with my journey and career, offering to help me to convert my VHS recordings of the movies I had acted in, though he didn't expect that it was 25 movies. We became good friends, brainstorming creative future projects. A few months later, I was going to meet him to collect my DVDs, but he didn't answer the phone. After couple of days I thought it was very unusual and became concerned. I kept calling. He was a person who would always, always answer his phone, or at the very least, would send a message saying, 'sorry, I'm flying, but I'll call you when I land.'

It was a Saturday when I got a call from a mutual friend who told me he had taken his life. It was so surreal. Ok universe – enough is enough! I couldn't sleep for a few nights. I was sitting having coffee in the morning with my husband, and said, 'Darlink, I'm going to create an event in support of men's mental health and suicide prevention with the motto *Men don't talk, boys don't cry. They rather die than cry.* And the event will be called The Men in Black Ball. Not as a sign of mourning, but because I love it when men wear black suits. They look empowered; they look a million dollars.

My husband just looked at me. 'Are you serious?' All these years later, I still feel passionate about creating awareness for men's mental health. 2008 was the inaugural ball, and now in 2024, it couldn't be more topical, more crucial and important to continue creating awareness about this. Unfortunately, suicide rates are growing. Men are four times more likely to take their lives than women. I've heard it so many times; the mothers, sisters and daughters always say, 'if only he'd told us he was struggling.' Often these men seem like the happiest people in the world.

Sometimes it's the bubbliest and most ridiculously happy

people on the outside, who are covering up something. Of course, we cannot think that everybody who looks happy and bubbly has a problem, neither must we assume quiet people are not content, or that very happy people don't have issues. There is no 'one size fits all' in mental health.

At the inaugural Men in Black Ball in 2008, Alan Carpenter, who was the Premier of Western Australia at the time, attended with his wife, AnnMarie. His office had called earlier asking if I would be happy to have Tim Marney as a testimonial speaker. He was the WA Under-Treasurer then and went on to become head of the mental health commission for a while. His journey was inspirational. Supporting Beyond Blue, the event was sold out, and the messages we received were incredible. Jeff Kennet, Chair of Beyond Blue, couldn't attend but recorded a message for the night.

I truly believe the Men in Black Ball, over the years, has been a big part in creating a real change in attitude and awareness about speaking openly about mental health. Back in 2008, nobody here was talking about it. The stigma had to be removed. MIB Ball started the conversation.

I am in awe at some of the speakers and the journeys they have shared over years. From returned soldiers who served in Afghanistan, leaders with PTSD, to FIFOs and people in the media and sporting champions, these people have been through so much and are speaking up to let others know they are not alone. I remember Heath Black, a Fremantle Dockers player, who went through absolute agony in his mental health journey. He told us he was like a lion in a cage, and 'if it wasn't for Men in Black, I wouldn't be standing here today. The journey of controlling my anxiety will never end. Ladies and gentlemen, I'm standing here because Barbara asked me, and I said *yes*. But before I came on stage, I was in the bathroom, almost throwing up.'

I get goosebumps whenever I think of the silence in a room when men talk about their journey. I remember Eric Ripper, then the Leader of the Opposition, agreeing to speak at the Ball. I had arranged for him to be interviewed by The West in the lead up to the ball, and Eric said, 'Barbara, please come to my office before the interview, what if they ask me things I don't want to say?' I replied, 'Just say what you choose to say, what makes you comfortable and what you think will help others. It's your journey, Eric.'

And Eric stood there on stage, the night of the Ball, and said, 'you know, when I said *yes* to Barbara, a lot of people who know me said I was crazy. But let me tell you, my anxiety sometimes took me to the situations where I felt paralysed, unable to walk out and address people, which is difficult in my profession. So, I need to share it, because I'm standing here now, and today I'm okay.'

I was approached one day by parents asking if they could bring their son, who was only 14, to the ball. Our events are normally over 18, as alcohol is served, but due to his mental health, they wanted him to see 'he wasn't alone'. I agreed he could attend, as long as they were in full supervision and ensured he wasn't drinking. After hearing some of the inspirational speakers, the young boy ran to me, also wearing his very smart black-tie suit by the way, saying 'Thank you. Barbara. I'm going to go to school on Monday and tell my friends to start opening up, because at the moment, we are all thinking we should be ashamed of how

Hello Darlink!

we're feeling, and that's just not true!'

My heartfelt thanks goes out to everyone who has attended, spoken, presented or performed over the years of at all of the Momentum events. I'm reminded of the wonderful Carmelo Pizzino from Dancing with The Stars, and his spectacular dancing and testimonial contribution to The Men in Black Ball in 2016.

You can watch Carmelo Pizzino's story on Hello Darlink! Talk Show. https://www.youtube.com/watch?v=F9g3ELeC9_g

Hello Darlink! talk show continues broadcasting messages of people that often survived the unsurvivable and have become messengers for change.

Thank you for watching and thank you for sharing xxx

With Anthony Mundine –
2022 Momentum Most Inspiring Man of the Year

1. Business leaders supporting Kiss violence against Women goodbye! campa[ign]
2. With Adrian Barich MC of the Men in Black Ball.
3. With Dana Vulin on "Hello Darlink!" set.
4. With Dame Quentin Bryce Governor General of Australia - IWD 2009.
5. With Jon Lewis MC & Maggie Beer AO, Guest Speaker.
6. With Annmarie and Alan Carpenter (WA Premier) at MIB Ball 2008.

With Hon Julie Bishop,
Momentum Most Inspiring Woman of the Year 2015

Chapter 16
INSPIRATIONAL WOMEN

In 2004, I launched the International Women's Day to Perth. These days there are many events across Perth on the day, but back then, nobody celebrated this day or at least very few did. Lisa Scaffidi, who had just become the first female Lord Mayor of Perth, was the guest speaker. I've been blessed to have some wonderful speakers and motivational women at my events.

In 2009, I wrote and asked The Honourable Dame Quentin Bryce AD CVO, at the time, Governor-General of Australia, to speak at our event and she said 'yes'. She flew from Canberra and spoke at the International Women's Day event. She flew in with her husband and it was her first public appearance in WA.

I also wrote to Prime Minister Kevin Rudd's wife, Therese Rein, and invited her to speak at the International Women's Day in 2008. She is a very successful businesswoman in her own right, with an incredible story, which I wanted her to share at my International Woman's Day event. She said 'Yes', and the advertising, publicity, and everything it takes to set up an event was organised, featuring Therese Rein as the keynote speaker. The newspapers and media were full of it. About ten days before the event, however, I had several missed calls from Canberra. There was a problem. 'Barbara. Barack Obama is arriving in Sydney and Therese and Kevin have to welcome him.' There were some sleepless nights, as we'd pre-sold tickets, based on Therese Rein being there. They were trying to work out any way that we could move times around for Therese to still attend.

Maggie Beer, celebrity chef and author, had just become the senior Australian of the year, so I reached out to Maggie explaining, why we'd only contacted her at such short notice, and she agreed to speak. So, Maggie Beer spoke at one of the biggest selling International Women's Day events. She was welcomed like a queen. Mothers with their children, waited outside the event, just to have their photo taken with her. She had actually flown in from Canberra, after having had dinner the night before with Kevin Rudd and Therese Rein. So, it all worked out very well. Another incredible story of successful speakers and beautiful people.

After what happened to Dana Vulin, the survivor of the vicious burn attack in 2012 and a number of other events that were part of the shocking statistics around violence against women, I knew it was time to bring some awareness to what was happening in our community.

In 2013, I invited Charlotte Dawson, who was based in Sydney at the time, to be guest speaker at the International Women's Day event. I was able to secure The Sunday Times as media sponsor with extensive coverage in the STM magazine. Charlotte Dawson, former model, TV personality, and judge on

Australia's Next Top Model, was making headlines after being bullied on social media to the extent of having made a suicide attempt.

The interview was arranged between Charlotte, who flew from Sydney, and the STM journalist. I was meeting Charlotte for the first time at the Duxton Hotel. My first impression when I saw Charlotte was how incredibly beautiful she was. She brought light to the room as she walked in. She insisted I stay for the whole interview.

I couldn't believe what I was hearing, the contradiction of Charlotte being so intelligent, strong and vulnerable at the same time. As I was leaving the hotel saying goodbye, Charlotte looked at me with such a deep sadness in her beautiful eyes; I thought, *I will remember this look forever.*

It was at the International Women's Day event in 2013, that we launched the campaign to *KISS VIOLENCE AGAINST WOMEN GOODBYE!* which was inspired by Charlotte's story, who had lost the battle with depression and took her life in February 2014. This campaign has been a huge part of my life for the last ten years and I'm so pleased for the momentum (*not sorry for the pun!*) it has created.

In 2015, we launched the *Most Inspiring Woman of the Year* award. In its inaugural year, Julie Bishop Foreign Minister of Australia, was nominated. She's a woman who walks her talk, and the way she represents our country, working in an environment which, let's face it, is still a bit of a boy's club – though hopefully not forever. She accepted the award, but we were told that unfortunately, due to her engagements in Canberra, she would not be there on the day. So, I emailed Julie asking her to film her 'thank you' speech to play at the event. We asked her to write her pledge, a message in support of our important awareness campaign, *Kiss Violence Against Women Goodbye*! campaign . The electronic copy was emailed to Julie Bishop's office.

I got a call the day before the event, to say Julie was able to change her plans and she would be arriving in Perth at 12:00pm on the day of the event. Julie arrived, looking smart and beautiful in her little black suit, and I thought of course she doesn't have the pledge, she wouldn't have had time sign. I was counting my blessings she was there, so I didn't ask her about it before going on stage. Funny the things that stick in our memory, but I remember she didn't even have a handbag. She delivered her speech ending with, 'Thank you to Barbara for everything she does for Australia.' Never mind thinking of me, but what Julie does for the cause and for the country is remarkable. Then she took her pledge from her pocket and kissed *Violence Against Women Goodbye!"* You can see the footage on YouTube.

Well, it seems my book has just about come to an end, but there are two very special women to mention before I finish; my Mum and my sister.

I'd like to honour my beautiful sister Ala; a sensitive and talented soul, who unfortunately had a weakness in her life. She died tragically, way too early, at the age of 39. The official diagnosis was a brain haemorrhage, but we knew she had a problem with drugs on the journey of her life. I was living in South Africa when I received the call from my mum to tell me what had happened. My sister struggled with mental health, and her journey certainly had an influence over the direction in which I have journeyed to support others, especially since I arrived in Australia.

Mums are always right!

Over all the years I lived outside of Poland, my Mum visited me every Christmas staying for 3 months, including Austria, Germany, France, South Africa and Australia. The last time she came to visit us in Perth was in 2018.

In 2019 my mum suffered irreversible anxiety. She never recovered and had to be hospitalised. I had two frantic years traveling three times a year to Poland to take care of her, while still running my events at the same time. I really don't know how I could have managed without the help of my Polish cousin Teresa, friend Iza, and my mum's friend, Lucyna, who at the age of 90, was visiting Mum in hospital in −18°C and helped to bathe her. The teamwork was a Manifesto of Sisterhood. God bless women power when they unite in crisis to help others.

My mother left this world in January 2020. I was lucky to be there. I was very close to her and not a day goes by where I don't think about her. What is strange, is that things your mum told you in the past will always reappear years later - and then you know …

Mums are aways right!

With my beautiful Mother in Perth

Hello Darlink! promotion at Yagan Square, Perth

Conclusion

SAY HELLO DARLINK! TO LIFE

The Hello Darlink! talk show was launched in 2012, inviting inspiring people to share their life changing stories, helping to make our world a better place. From celebrities to unsung heroes, episodes engage in conversation with guests from all walks of life including authors, entrepreneurs, cancer and domestic violence survivors, sports stars, fashion icons and emerging artists.

I'm linking people all over the world through my show, via YouTube and Foxtel, so that those who may be going through difficult times, know they are not alone.

The life changing journeys include :

'Stories From Under the Blanket,' - because no-one should have to feel that they must hide their feelings, and I will never know how many lives have been touched by journeys shared.

'Talk about - Walk About' - introducing indigenous

Australians who walked their way to success leaving footprints for generations to come.

'Recipes For Life' - introducing success and game changing journeys.

I feel so blessed to be able to share the inspirational stories of so many remarkable individuals, but of course, there are always several stand-out experiences.

I did an interview with Samantha Sepulveda from USA who was in Western Australia to receive an award. When I did the interview with her, we called it the 'Sexiest Cop Alive' because, as well as being an incredible personality, she is so beautiful. Her main job was as a cop in New York City, as well as being celebrated lingerie model - I'm talking HOT. She has 400,000 Instagram followers, and after our interview, she was featured in the New York Post, and has appeared in many further interviews.

I enjoyed interviewing John Jarratt, star of the movie *Wolf Creek*. John was in Perth to launch a new movie he had filmed in WA. The interview was filmed at Backlot Studios, and I was very conscious of not only talking about *Wolf Creek*, because everybody sees him as that character. When we finished, John said, 'This was the best interview I've ever done.'

Another story close to my heart, is of the beautiful Australian fashion designer Ruth Tarvydas, who was an absolute icon of fashion for 25 years. I met her when I first arrived in Australia and she dressed me for all my balls, including my first Pink Ribbon Ball in 2003. We'd been friends for some time when I launched the Hello Darlink! talk show. I always wanted to interview Ruth because her life journey was incredibly inspirational. She was a self-made icon with an international career. She was the first to dress Kim Kardashian, even before Kim became a worldwide name! Instagram was still a novelty, but even then, I remember Ruth telling me in an interview, 'Barbara, if you think influencers or social media icons don't work hard, you're wrong … it never stops.'

Ruth was very hardworking and has dressed some of the world's biggest celebrities. She designed the famous red dress worn by Rebecca Twigley, the then girlfriend (now wife) of WA sporting hero, Chris Judd. Ruth told me about the famous white dress worn by Lady Sonia McMahon when she accompanied her husband the Australian Prime Minister to a dinner hosted by President Richard Nixon. The daring dress for those days wowed and scandalised the White House in 1971. Ruth reconstructed the dress especially for me to wear at the International Women's Day that Ruth attended in 2018. Finally, after years of asking Ruth to do an interview, she sent me a message giving me the date and time we could sit down and talk. 'I have two hours free on that day,' she said, 'we can do the interview then.' She was so beautiful and charismatic, with wonderful energy. She was so trustworthy too; she didn't want to see the script. 'Darling, it's the only way to do interviews.' At the time, she was on top of the world. I remember saying to her, 'wow, your life *was* amazing.' She said, 'what do you mean? Was? My life continues to be amazing.'

She had created a collection called Ruthless Ruth. I asked her, 'Who is the real Ruth?'

'The real Ruth is a survivor,' she replied. That was in September 2013. The interview was released on YouTube and Foxtel. In May 2014, Ruth died. I was walking down King Street, past where

Ruth's shop had been until high rentals had forced her to close it. I was thinking of Ruth when the phone rang. It was one of Ruth's young friends who used to model and work for her. She was in tears and asked, 'have you heard about Ruth?' It was awful.... She had committed suicide by jumping from her apartment building.

The UK Daily Mail contacted me because the story had made international headlines. They saw my interview and wanted to use the excerpt of 'Real Ruth – the Survivor.' I agreed, because my biggest gratitude in what I do, is to continue to share the journey of a diverse selection of inspiring and motivational people, knowing we are all human and how the awareness of these stories can support the journey of so many others. My main intention through my show, is to help others.

It's also interesting how the world has become so small. I met with the Daily Mail journalist from the UK who had worked on the story of Ruth, several years later when I covered the Nazi Gold Train story in Poland!

In August 2015 I was visiting my mum in Warsaw, Poland, as I did each summer. One day, I received a phone call from a producer friend in Perth who was very excited. 'Barbara, you've got to cover the Nazi train story on your show. The whole world is talking about it. They're saying it's in the south of Poland.' The Nazis had buried trains from World War II in tunnels, containing Nazi gold, papers, treasures and maybe even the amber from the famous Amber Room in Russia that had disappeared from a palace in St. Petersburg. 'They have journalists coming from all over the world to see if it's real or not.'

I was stunned. How would I organise that? I was just visiting my mum! 'I don't have a crew in Poland or any contacts,'

I replied. 'What are you talking about? Just find the crew,' he continued, 'it's you, Barbara, and this is a huge story. Just find a crew.' It was August, the middle of the long school holidays, and everyone was travelling. I called production companies and TV companies, but the response was the same everywhere. 'Talk to us in September.' There was nothing available.

However, one morning, I had been to the dentist, but had forgotten to pick up my mum's prescription from the chemist, so had to go back. I considered not going, as it was raining, but as a good daughter, I walked back the way I'd come, when I heard; 'Excuse me Madam. Excuse me, but we're filming here, and you are in the picture.' That's when I saw the crew, and realised that if I hadn't backtracked, I'd never have seen them. I asked, 'Guys, what are you recording?' 'We're shooting a TV series … Why?' 'Well, I'm Barbara from Hello Darlink! TV in Australia, and I really need a crew.' I'm introduced to the director, who says, 'well, obviously not right now, but let's exchange numbers, okay? We will call you later?' Within days, I had a crew. We are still friends today and have produced several projects together.

We drove to the south of Poland and stayed in one of the oldest and most beautiful castles in Europe, because that was the area where the Nazi gold train was located. There were countries from all over the world doing live coverage and for Deutsche Wounds – a German documentary production. Every morning as were walking down to cover the story, everyone would say their hello's; Bonjour, Guten Tag, Good Morning, and everyone remembered me with my, *Hello Darlink*! They obviously didn't expect me, from an Australian talk show, to be speaking Polish, but I was everyone's friend because I could translate and speak with the researchers and locals. I had the wonderful experience of interviewing an incredible older gentleman who had initiated the whole movement. We interviewed him in his house, and he told me how, as a child, he saw with his own eyes, people being shot across the road during the war … and then being buried there. He had spent 60 years researching the truth behind the Nazi Gold train.

I met the journalist from the Daily Mail at a breakfast press conference. We were all introducing ourselves and saying where we were from, 'I'm from Hello Darlink! TV,' I say. And he replied, 'I know you! We used an excerpt of your interview with Ruth Tarvydas a few years ago.'

Another truly inspirational person I have interviewed, three times now, is Dana Vulin. As I've said so many times, everyone should watch this interview. Whenever you feel sorry for yourself or too tired to pick yourself up and do something, you should watch Dana Vulin's story. Dana received third-degree burns to over half her body, after being set alight with methylated spirits, when a women broke into her apartment and wrongly accused her of having affair with her husband. I am in awe of her amazing strength and love of life. Her first public interview was on *Hello Darlink! Talk Show,* and it was the first time she was without her mask.

Dana's first public event, where she was without her body bandage and mask, was at the 2014 Pink Ribbon Ball. I remember all the media fighting to be there. The first interview with Dana is short, but has over half-a-million views and still continues gaining views from all over the world.

I am not able to mention all the special guests on my show

over the years. One remarkable interview recorded with my Polish crew in Poland was with Ewa Blaszczyk, a celebrated Polish actress who's life took an unexpectedly tragic turn in 2000. Her 4 year old daughter Ola, one of twins, choked fatally by swallowing a pill and fell into coma till present.

Ewa Blaszczyk used the tragedy to dedicate her life to research, reaching out to some of the worlds biggest specialists and launching a Clinic called Budzik (Alarm Clock) in Warsaw in 2013, with the purpose of bringing children in a coma back to life. At the time of my interview 37 children had woken up through the clinic and that number is now in excess of 100.

This story is another testament to a most remarkable woman of strength and courage, proving that anything is possible if you persist and reach for the stars.

Thank you to all my guests for their courage to share their life changing journeys, that help to make our world a better place.

Thank you to all my viewers for watching and remember to say, HELLO DARLINK! to life.

Image: Chris Huzzard. // Kisses to you.

Filmography

BARBARA NIELSEN

1998 Prostytutki

1995 Soweto Green

1990 Schweitzer

1985 Tranches de vie

1984 Year of the Jellyfish

1984 Non-Stop Trouble with My Double

1983 La fiancée qui venait du froid

1983 Monaco Franze – Der ewige Stenz

1978 Kameliendame

1977 Die Unternehmungen des Herrn Hans

1977 Hajka

1976 Derrick

1976 Alle Jahre wieder: Die Famille Semmeling

1976 Auch Mimosen wollen blühen

1975 Ich denk', mich tritt eim Pferd

1975 Armchair Cinema

1975 Das Rückendekollete

1974 Zwei im 7. Himmel

1974 Schwarzwaldfahrt aus Liebeskummer

1973 Stawiam na Tolka Banana

1973 Das Wandern ist Herrn Müllers Lust

1973 Alter Kahn und junge Liebe

1972 Siedem czerwonych roz, czyli Benek kwiaciarz o sobie I o innych

1972 Anatomia milosci

Source: https://www.imdb.com/name/nm0073564/

Aus Italien kam die Nachricht, daß der berühmte polnische Filmregisseur Roman Polanski wieder heiraten will. Seine Auserwählte soll seiner ermordeten Frau Sharon Tate zum Verwechseln ähnlich sehen und Barbara Nielsen heißen. Zu frau sagte Barbara:

Roman Polanski und ich sind nur gute Freunde

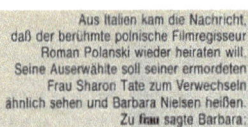

Roman Polanski heiratet wieder! Diese Nachricht machte schnell die Runde durch die römische Schickeria. Während des Theaterfestivals in Spoleto/Italien soll der bekannte Regisseur sogar gesagt haben: „Endlich habe ich die Richtige gefunden!"

Er meinte damit die blonde Barbara Nielsen, von deren Seite er während des Festivals nicht wich. Barbara sieht seiner ersten Frau Sharon Tate, die im August 1969 grausam ermordet wurde, verblüffend ähnlich.

In Rom wird erzählt, daß Polanski bereits das Aufgebot bestellt und bei einem offiziellen Festessen gesagt habe: „Ich sehne mich nach einer Frau, die immer für mich da ist. Die keine Karriere machen. Es genügt, wenn einer von uns beiden berühmt ist."

Man sah Roman, der lange Zeit den Tod seiner Frau nicht verwinden konnte, schon oft an der Seite schöner Frauen. Und Hochzeitsgerüchte gab es ebenfalls mehrfach. frau wollte wissen, ob diesmal etwas Wahres an den Gerüchten ist und fragte die hübsche Barbara.

„Nein", sagte sie spontan. „Davon stimmt kein Wort. Ich erzähle Ihnen aber gern, wie es zu diesen Gerüchten gekommen ist. Ich selbst habe an Roman Polanski vor einiger Zeit einen Brief geschrieben, weil ich gern mit ihm arbeiten möchte. Daraufhin lud er mich nach Italien ein.

So lernten wir uns kennen und fanden uns sympathisch. Ich bin ja auch aus Polen. Es ist klar, daß wir glücklich waren, in unserer Muttersprache miteinander reden zu können. Es stimmt, daß wir häufig ausgegangen und befreundet sind.

In drei Wochen fliege ich von München aus wieder nach Rom. Roman will Probeaufnahmen mit mir machen. Drücken Sie mir die Daumen, daß alles gut geht."

Ich drücke der sympathischen Polin, die noch einige Schwierigkeiten mit der

Barbara Nielsen mit Partner Roy Black in dem Film „Schwarzwaldfahrt aus Liebeskummer". Die blonde Polin, die Polanskis erster Frau Sharon Tate verblüffend ähnlich sieht, ist sehr ehrgeizig. Rechts: Roman Polanski mit Sharon Tate, wenige Monate vor ihrer Ermordung.

Barbara Nielsen
165/36-38
89-60-89
blond, blaugrün

kd München

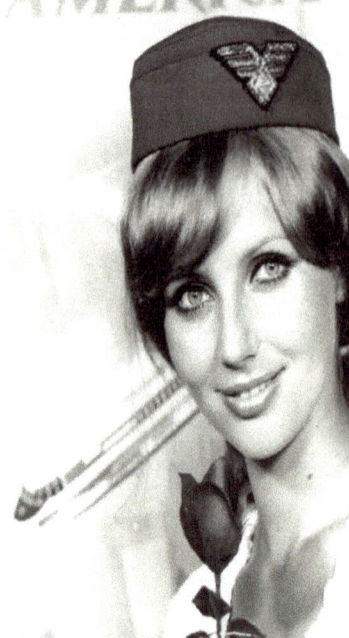

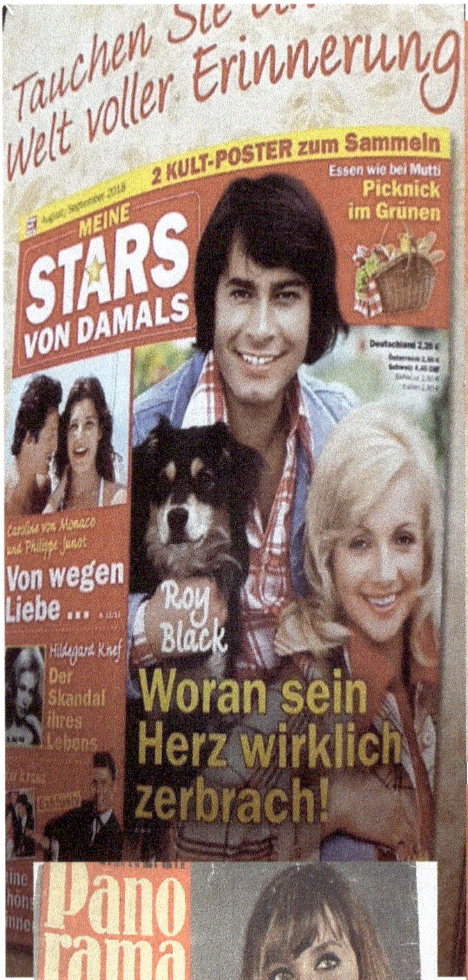
Tauchen Sie ein
Welt voller Erinnerung
2 KULT-POSTER zum Sammeln
Essen wie bei Mutti
Picknick
im Grünen
MEINE
STARS
VON DAMALS
Caroline von Monaco
und Philippe Junot
Von wegen
Liebe ...
Hildegard Knef
Der
Skandal
ihres
Lebens
Roy
Black
Woran sein
Herz wirklich
zerbrach!

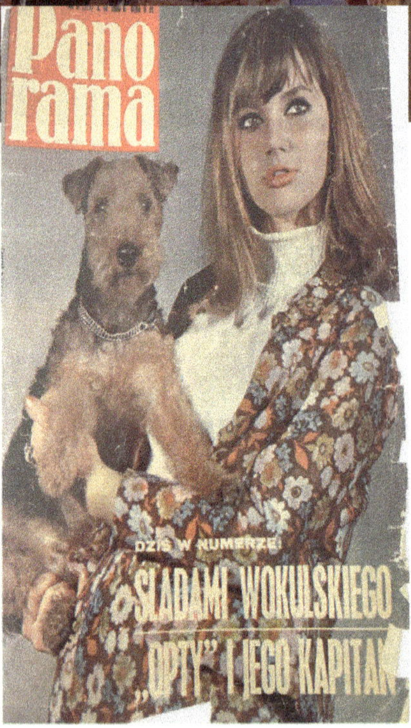
Pano
rama
DZIS W NUMERZE:
SLADAMI WOKULSKIEGO
„OPTY" I JEGO KAPITAN

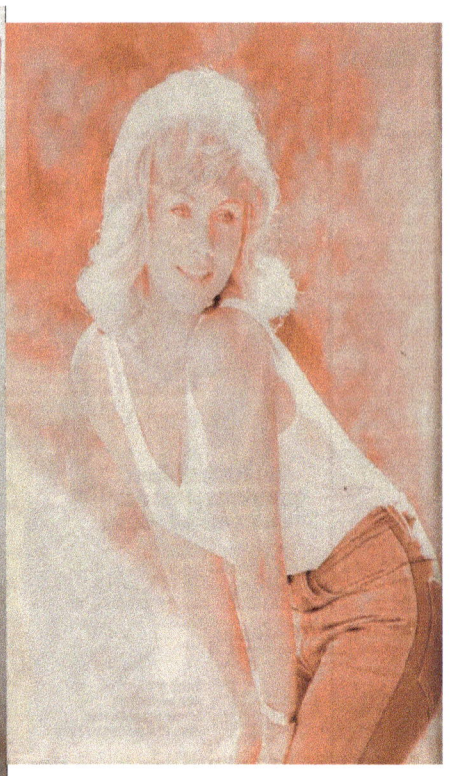

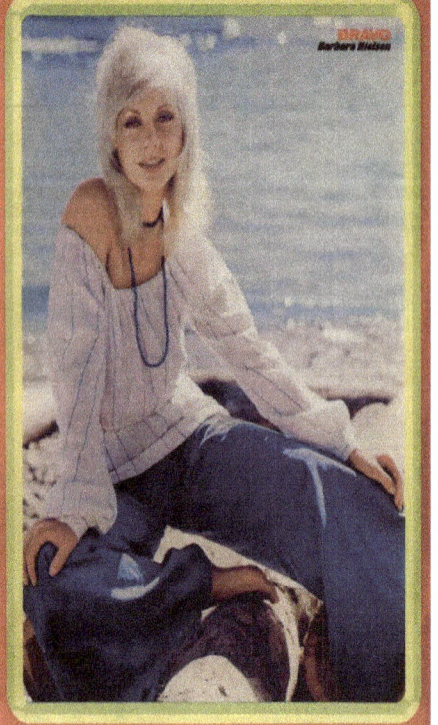

www.ingramcontent.com/pod-product-compliance
Lightning Source LLC
Chambersburg PA
CBHW062050290426
44109CB00027B/2779